McSWEENEY'S
PRESENTS...

THE GOODS

EDITED BY MAC BARNETT

AND BRIAN McMULLEN

WHAT IS THE GOODS?

THE GOODS is a collection of games, puzzles, and hard-to-classify diversions from some of the best artists and writers around. We dreamed up THE GOODS as a weekly all-ages feature for newspapers, and we're excited that forty-four installments have been transformed into the unusual book you're now holding.

This book is for people who love joy, labyrinths, fortune-telling, bears, glaring penguins, and made-up words. It is not for people who love symmetrical shapes. Our brilliant GOODS-makers were given strange and small spaces in which to work — and not a lot of time, either — and it is these constraints that lend the material a peculiar glory. We hope you like it.

—The Editors

HOW TO DRAW A PELICAN!

Follow these **5** steps to make your very own feathered friend!

Those big beaks sure hold a lot of spaghetti!

DRAW HERE! | **1** | **2** | **3** | **4** | **5**

Here's a spot where you can draw. Now let's get started!

Make 3 curved lines like above. These will make his wing!

Make another curve next to the others, to be his big belly!

Make a big "U" shape over the belly, and add lines for feet.

Put a lid on the "U" to make a beak, and finish the wing with a line.

Now add circles and dots for eyes, and an upside-down "U" for his little head!

A BLUE WHALE'S HEART IS AS BIG AS A CAR!

JOKE TIME! HOW DO YOU CARRY A TUNA? Just singa the cana! you can!

FISH FACES

The crew of the USS Bacon each look just like one of these fish! Can you match them up?

U.S.S. BACON

SCUBA MAZE

Start

Oh NO!

Finish

Help Sally & Sammy Scuba find their way to the toys lost in the sunken ship! But watch out for sharks!

AN OCTOPUS HAS ABOUT 240 SUCTION CUPS ON EACH ARM. THAT'S 1,920 SUCTION CUPS TOTAL!

PELICAN SPECIALIST: KEVIN CORNELL
MAZE SPECIALIST: PETER DALKNER
FISH-FACE SPECIALIST: MATTHEW SUTTER

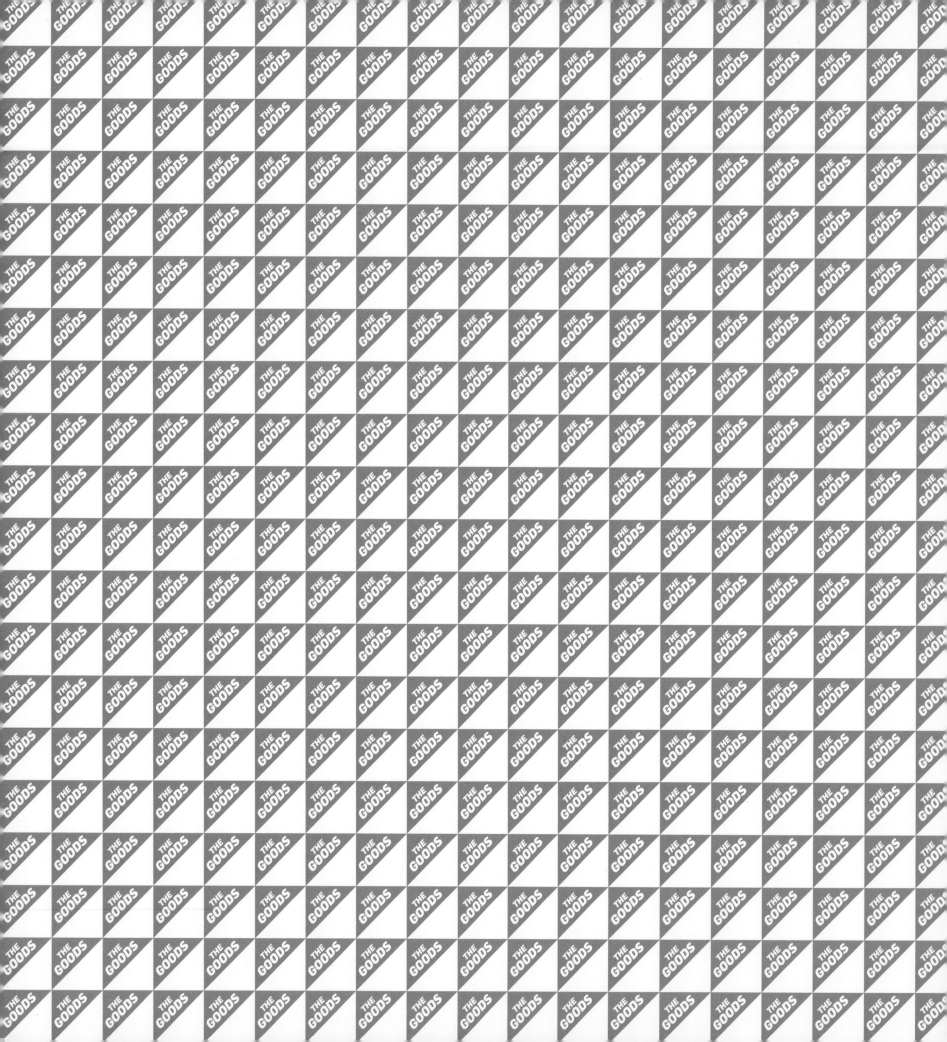

THE GOODS

NINE THINGS NINE PRESIDENTS NEVER, EVER SAID

"I wish I had purchased more video games."
—George Washington

"True love is the kind one hides, hoards, and keeps all to oneself. Any love shared with others is not love at all."
—John Adams

"Can I appoint myself to the Supreme Court? Is that possible? Let's look into this."
—Thomas Jefferson

"I once built a cage, then stole the cage from myself to give back to myself. I regret doing that."
—James Madison

"You guys, I'm feeling, like, so totally freaked out and scared right now."
—James Monroe

"If you need me, I'll be at Tammy's nail salon. It's on 4th Street."
—John Q. Adams

"Sure I'd like to have thighs five times as long. But how would I tie my shoes?"
—Andrew Jackson

"Tell Canada they can have Montana if they give me a brownie of some kind. No nuts."
—Martin Van Buren

"I sleep with slices of Swiss cheese on my eyes because I am the White House's best mousetrap."
—Zachary Taylor

THE DARE CORNER

V.P. ANSWERS:
A2, B3, C1, D4

1. Put a tie on the First Dog and bring him to a cabinet meeting. Introduce the dog as the Secretary of Treats.

2. Use the word "forcefield" three times during a speech to Congress.

3. Prank call the president of Iceland (but double check with the Secretary of State and make sure he doesn't have caller ID).

4. Make a big bowl of oatmeal and walk around asking people to try it.

ENTER →

EXIT →

HOW MANY THINGS can YOU FIND WRONG WITH THIS PICTURE?!

ANSWER:
THERE'S NOTHING WRONG WITH THIS PICTURE. THIS PICTURE IS AWESOME.

BUT WHAT ABOUT THE VICE PRESIDENTS?

MATCH THESE VICE PRESIDENTS AND FACTS.

A. CHARLES G. DAWES

B. HENRY A. WALLACE

C. JOHN TYLER

D. WILLIAM RUFUS DEVANE KING

1. WAS NOT BURIED IN U.S. SOIL.

2. WROTE THE MUSIC FOR THE 1958 #1 POP SINGLE "IT'S ALL IN THE GAME" BY TOMMY EDWARDS.

3. DEVELOPED THE FIRST COMMERCIALLY VIABLE HYBRID-SEED CORN, THE FOUNDATION FOR ALMOST ALL THE CORN WE EAT TODAY.

4. WAS NICKNAMED "MISS NANCY" AND "AUNT FANCY" DUE TO HIS FLAMBOYANT STYLE OF DRESS.

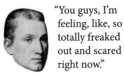

"V.P. FACTS" COMPILED BY J. RYAN STRADAL; SHAWN HARRIS, ILLUSTRATOR
"PRESIDENT QUOTES" BY BRIAN McMULLEN & JORDAN BASS
"DARES" BY MICHAELANNE PETRELLA & MAC BARNETT
"WASHINGTON" BY BRIAN BIGGS
"LINCOLN" BY ADAM REX

THE GOODS

You! Earthling! Name the COUNTRIES in which we can find & protect your planet's FINEST buildings before they are destroyed by **GIANT CYCLOPIC ANTS** from Pluto!!!

EMPIRE STATE BUILDING

TAIPEI 101

BURJ KHALIFA

HAVE YOU GUIDED THE DO-GOODER ALIENS CORRECTLY?!?
Confirming your answers only requires a bit of PERSPECTIVE...
Cut out this section & lay it flat on the table. Then close one eye and look at the buildings: the correct answers will be revealed.

FINGER COMIX! Ask a grown-up to cut out these finger puppets & tape them around your fingers so you can perform your own **Elephant & Piggie** skits for your pals!

ELEPHANT & PIGGIE COMIX!
by Mo Willems!

copyright © 2011 Mo Willems

Zonk! Blaaarp! Beeeeeep!

Boopy-Boopy-Boopy! BRRRRINGG!

Hello? I'm sorry, you have the wrong number. Bye!

Murrff! Blurp! Wango! Saxophone.

THEY get a comics page!?! Typical.

THE DARE CORNER

1. Give the family pet a new name for a day.
2. Pretend that your leg was bitten by a dinosaur and ask your parents for the life-saving powers of cookies.
3. Attach the largest fruit you can find to your head using string or tape. Pretend you have two heads.

TREASURE HUNT
START
FINISH

CONNECT THE WORDS

HOW TO PLAY:
This puzzle is half word search, half connect-the-dots. To solve it, find & connect — in order — the words of the provided sentence.

FIND & CONNECT THESE WORDS TO REVEAL A PICTURE:
"ZEUS IS IN A REAL GOOD MOOD TODAY — PLEASE DON'T BOTHER HIM."

CUP RUST IN
HUG ZOO
IS NOT
DO MYTHS
DOGS ZEAL
BROTHER
TOES POP
ME DROP
SO
MOO GOON JOB
REAL
TOAST NO A LEAN
JELLY
ZEUS LOUD
BOTHER
HIM PEALS
ROOT
SO
FANGS GET
HANDLE
TOUR BEE
PLANS ZAPS MOOD
BREAD GOOD STEELY
DENT DRIFT
YOURS TOAST
GUM PLEASE MUSHY
MAN BOILED
BOOT
DON'T
ENTER OH GEL
SURE ROOSTER FLAP
SISTER
STUNT DEPOT
ZOOM
BRIGHT TODAY
HE

"ELEPHANT & PIGGIE COMIX" BY MO WILLEMS
"CONNECT THE WORDS" BY BRIAN McMULLEN
"CYCLOPIC ANTS" BY SHAWN HARRIS
"PIRATE MAZE" BY DAN SANTAT

3

RASPUTIN
(Some folks just called him THE MAD MONK!)
PAPER DOLLS

MEET RASPUTIN! Grigori Rasputin was born 22 January 1869, in Russia, and he became the personal advisor to the Czarina Alexandra. Many people thought Rasputin was a faith healer, and he treated the symptoms of the young Czarevich Alexis's hemophilia. But things didn't turn out so well for Rasputin in the end. His enemies lured him into the basement of the Moika Palace and fed him poisoned food and wine. He survived the poisoning, so his murderers shot him—FOUR TIMES—but he STILL wouldn't die. So this gang of men clubbed him repeatedly, but he STILL was alive so they drowned him, and that's how he finally died. While there are a lot of tall tales about THE MAD MONK, sadly, none involve him being a pioneer or an astronaut. But with this special d-luxe CUT 'N' PLAY paper doll, you can dress ol' Rasputin up in all sorts of getups. *Do svidaniya!*

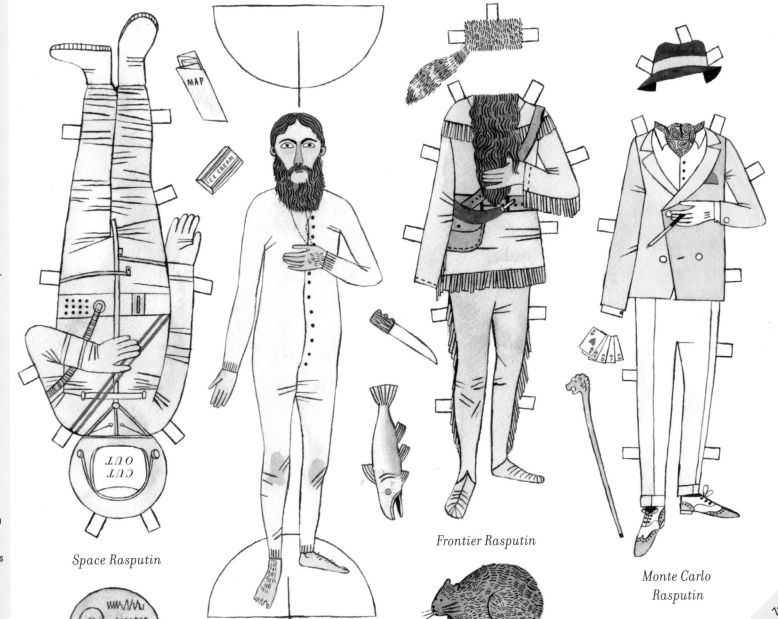

Space Rasputin

Frontier Rasputin

Monte Carlo Rasputin

*We recommend pasting Rasputin (and his stand)
to a piece of cardboard. He'll last longer.*

NEW ANSWERS TO OLD RIDDLES

The best way to look smart is to stump someone with a riddle. The quickest way to feel dumb is to tell a riddle to somebody who already knows the answer. To ensure your success, we provide new answers to old riddles.

THE RIDDLE

A boy and his father are in a car accident. The father dies, but the boy is taken to the hospital for emergency surgery. A gray-haired, bespectacled surgeon takes one look at the patient and says, "I cannot operate on this boy. He is my son." How is this possible?

THE OLD ANSWER

The doctor is the boy's mother.

THE NEW ANSWER

Five minutes before the boy arrived at the hospital, the gray-haired, bespectacled doctor had been in the Surgeons' Lounge, swapping hilarious surgery stories with his surgeon friends. This one surgeon was telling a really funny story—it was about a man who swallowed not just one but two 60-watt lightbulbs (classic surgeon humor)—and everybody was laughing so hard they were crying, and all the surgeons who wore glasses had to take them off to wipe their eyes. Just then the gray-haired doctor was urgently summoned to the operating room. He was in such a hurry that he grabbed the wrong pair of glasses. Oh, man! The gray-haired doctor couldn't see anything. He was nearsighted, and these glasses, well they belonged to someone who was farsighted! And this doctor's eyesight was so terrible that he mistook the boy for his own son—although in fairness the two boys had the same hair color and similar facial features. Anyway, the glasses got switched and the boy survived and today he owns and operates a very successful pizzeria (one of the toppings he uses is nettles, which sounds weird but turns out to be delicious), and he's thinking of opening up a second restaurant across town.

SING SONG PLUG SPAN DAWN SNUG SPAN SPUN RING SHOW PAWN LONG YARN SIGN SPUN DARN
SPAN YAWN SNUG SPAM YARN SPUD SING SONG SONG SPUN PAWN SONG SONG SPAM SANG SONG

ALTERNATE NEW ANSWER
Zombie surgeon.

"NEW ANSWERS TO OLD RIDDLES" BY MAC BARNETT
"RASPUTIN PAPER DOLLS" BY CARSON ELLIS
RASPUTIN BIOGRAPHY BY COLIN MELOY
"FIND THE WORD" BY BRIAN McMULLEN

4

TIME TO TEST THE LIMITS OF → YOUR BODY

AT YOUR AGE, GRAY HAIR AND TOOTHLESSNESS MUST SEEM A DISTANT IMPOSSIBILITY, BUT YOUR BODY DOES HAVE ITS LIMITS.
PRACTICE EACH OF THESE TESTS ONCE A DAY TO MAKE YOURSELF MORE POWERFUL.

1 → BRAIN TEST

Everyone knows smart people are nerds. It's a proven, scientific fact. A nerd proved it using math or something. But thanks to nerds we have stuff like video games, Facebook, and WD-50 (a restaurant you'll eat at when you're older). Now all those nerds are rich off their brains. You could get rich off yours, too!

STEP 1: PICK THE LONGEST, MOST BORING ARTICLE IN A NEWSPAPER. (PROBABLY IN WORLD NEWS.)
STEP 2: READ IT AGAIN AND AGAIN UNTIL YOU CAN FINISH IN UNDER 45 SECONDS.
STEP 3: DO IT ALL AGAIN, BUT READ ALOUD IN A LANGUAGE YOU DON'T SPEAK. FINNISH, MAYBE.

2 → LUNG TEST

Hopefully you aren't a smoker, because this next test requires a strong pair of lungs. Plus, smoking gives you cancer.

STEP 1: LYING ON YOUR BACK, PLACE A SHEET OF NEWSPAPER ON YOUR FACE.
STEP 2: BLOW A STREAM OF AIR, LEVITATING THE PAPER FOR 10 SECONDS, 15 SECONDS, AND CONTINUING UNTIL 3 HOURS. (YOU'RE A KID, YOU'VE GOT THE TIME.) ALSO, DON'T BLACK OUT.

3 → MUSCLE TEST

Bodybuilders spend all day trying to make their muscles big enough to hide their emotional troubles. It doesn't work.

STEP 1: USE YOUR NECK MUSCLES TO PUNCH A HOLE THROUGH A PIECE OF PAPER WITH YOUR HEAD. LOOK FIRST TO BE SURE THERE IS NO WALL BEHIND THE PAPER.

OH BOY, OH BOY!

THIS NEXT THING WILL TAKE YOUR BODY TO EXTREME LIMITS

BONUS TEST

The average hawk thinks his eyes are better than yours. Prove that jerk he's wrong.

STEP 1: BEGIN READING ALL THIS TEXT.
STEP 2: CONTINUE READING REGARDLESS OF HOW SMALL IT BECOMES. DON'T TURN BACK.
STEP 3: EVEN IF THE TEXT GETS AS SMALL AS THIS, YOU SHOULD STILL KEEP READING IT.
STEP 4: TAKE A MOMENT TO REST YOUR EYES, BECAUSE THIS REALLY ISN'T GETTING ANY BIGGER.
STEP 5: OK, RESTED UP? GOOD, BECAUSE LOOK AT THIS TEXT. SERIOUSLY.
STEP 6: THIS WAS A PATIENCE TEST AND YOU PASSED!

MOST PEOPLE DON'T SEE IT, BUT **Percy and PEARL ARE (fraternal) TWINS!** CAN YOU SPOT THEIR 10 SIMILARITIES?

TRUE LOVE QUIZ

Are you and your crush made for each other? Here are a few questions you can ask to find out. Circle your answers ahead of time, and if your crush's answers match yours, science says that you have chosen the perfect match.

IF IT WERE MY BIRTHDAY, WHAT WOULD YOU BUY ME?
✓ A bouquet of vegetables   ✓ Thousands & thousands of birds
✓ Limited-edition collectible football plate with gold rim   ✓ Trunk full of chicken bones & hairballs

IF WE WENT ON A DATE, WHERE WOULD YOU TAKE ME?
✓ Spelunking   ✓ Napkin store   ✓ Aquarium gift shop   ✓ Haunted softball field

IF YOU HAD TO WATCH ONE OF THESE MOVIES WITH ME, WHICH WOULD YOU CHOOSE?
✓ Anything with a cartoon hamster   ✓ A movie about sword-fighting tacos that play soccer
✓ A documentary about soil   ✓ A film about dancing being illegal

CONNECT THE WORDS

HOW TO PLAY: This puzzle is half word search, half connect-the-dots. To solve it, find & connect—in order—the words of the provided sentences.

FIND & CONNECT THESE WORDS TO REVEAL A PICTURE: "MATH HOMEWORK IS ONE OF MY VERY FAVORITE THINGS. GO AHEAD AND LAUGH. NOBODY'S MORE IRRATIONAL THAN I AM."

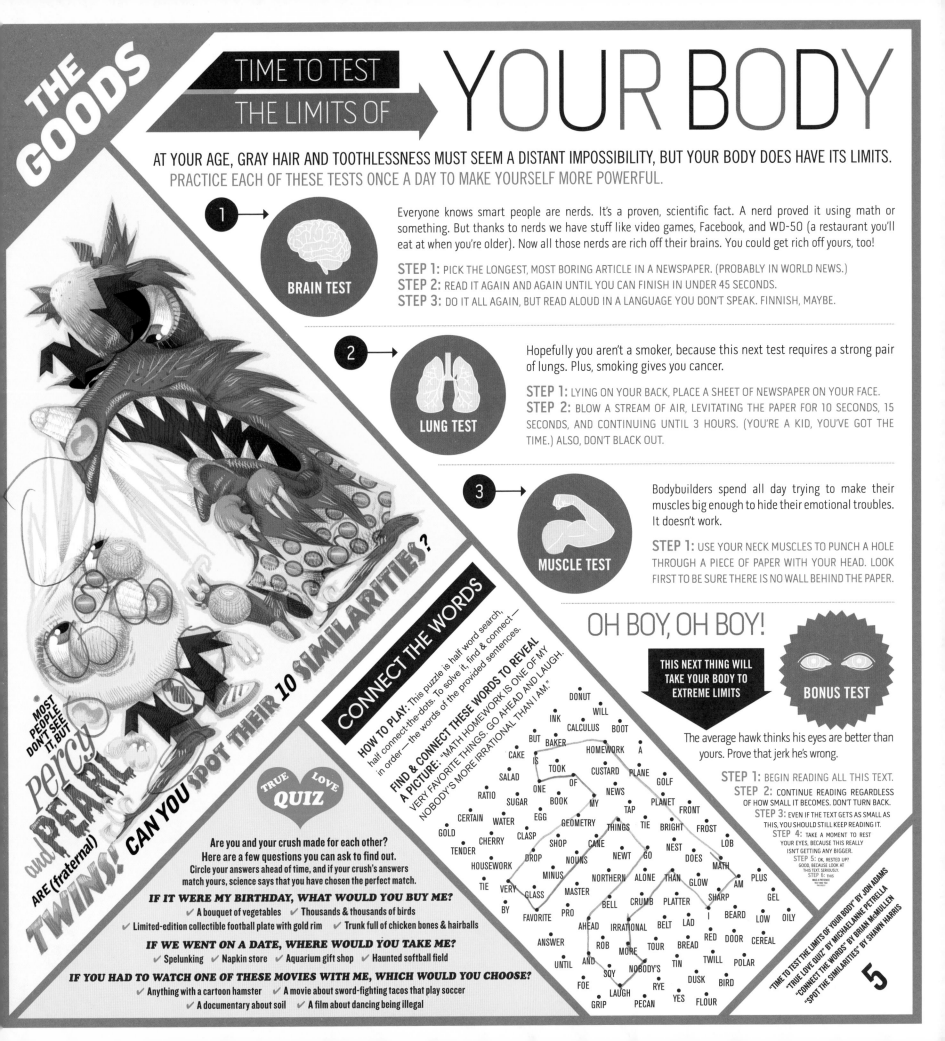

"TIME TO TEST THE LIMITS OF YOUR BODY" BY JON ADAMS
"TRUE LOVE QUIZ" BY MICHAELANNE PETRELLA
"CONNECT THE WORDS" BY BRIAN McMULLEN
"SPOT THE SIMILARITIES" BY SHAWN HARRIS

5

THE GOODS

HERO MILK

THE BACK STORY ON HERO MILK

Every spring, natives of the Blue Turtle Archipelago launch their fishing boats and paddle far out to sea in search of the gold-finned pyramidfish. The currents around those islands are strong, and carry man-eating sharks whose teeth tear the hulls of even the best-made canoes. Here is how the islanders prepare for their journey: they fell a tall banana tree and drag it to the snowy peak of a nearby volcano. Once the bananas freeze, they make a slurry in a giant mortar and pestle carved from lava rocks. They drink the mixture, called Hero Milk, from the skulls of monkeys, toasting to the trials ahead. One skull-full fuels three days' heavy paddling. Plus it's delicious.

MAKE YOUR OWN HERO MILK

• Let two bananas sit until they turn completely black and mushy.
• Remove the peel and freeze the banana mush overnight. If you don't have a giant mortar and pestle, use a blender and mix the frozen bananas with:

1 CUP OF MILK	1 SPOON OF HONEY
2 DATES (PITS REMOVED)	1 THIMBLE OF VANILLA
1 HANDFUL OF SALTED CASHEWS	

• Use a cup if you don't have a monkey skull.

Tales of Transparency:
THE CASE OF THE INVISIBLE MONSTER

HELP BRING HIM BACK!

I JUST DON'T SEE IT...

THAT IS WHY YOU FAIL.

Something has gone terribly wrong at the MONSTER INSTITUTE OF TECHNOLOGY. One of the post-docs in the SECRET PROJECTS LAB reached for his morning energy drink and accidentally gulped down a beaker of INVISI-FUR® POTION instead! Monsters are perfectly lovely creatures, as you know, but when they're invisible they are a bit of a menace in a lab environment. Can you help me make my colleague visible again? You can use your REVISIBILATOR if you like. Or a pen. Either way works.

AWWWW CRUMB-STEAK!

Poor Farmer Flinders forgot to count his chickens before they hatched... Can you give him a hand?

Hi, reader. I've spelled a five-letter word that means "short and stocky" by circling one letter in each row. Can you spell a five-letter word that means "tall and thin" by circling one letter in each row? (Note: there are two possible answers. Can you find them both? Look hard!)

```
  R S X P B L E W V C A T
  C X N A O B M S N L A X D O
  U R N A F N T U G K B
  M N E Y A M K T U Y
```

"HERO MILK" BY ERIC WOLFINGER & MAC BARNETT & WALTER GREEN
"THE CASE OF THE INVISIBLE MONSTER" BY STEFAN G. BUCHER
"AWWWW CRUMB-STEAK!" BY SHAWN HARRIS
SPELLING GAME BY BRIAN McMULLEN

SOLUTION TO THE CHICKEN-COUNTING GAME: 40. ★ SOLUTION TO THE SPELLING GAME: "LANKY" AND "RANGY" ARE BOTH CORRECT.

THE GOODS

NOW PRESENTING
Uncle Jon's Believe It!
(OR ACTUALLY MAYBE YOU SHOULDN'T!)

TEACHERS around the world believe that if you do not give a Valentine to everyone else in your class, a little chubby kid with wings wearing diapers **will shoot you with his tiny bow and arrow!**

VAMPIRE POODLES are some of the most dangerous animals in the world. They have forked tongues and **can spit pink poison 20 inches (50 cm)!**

SCIENTISTS have recently translated the mysterious songs of the humpback whale (Megaptera novaeangliae). But they aren't telling anyone, **because it's mostly cursing!**

THE DARE CORNER

1. Answer the phone with a French accent for the entire day.
2. Pour five cups of water on your head while singing "Singing in the Rain."
3. Call a pet store and ask them to please name one of their animals after you.

VISION QUEST!

While most of us have seen an ice cream cone riding a motorcycle, it is EXTREMELY rare to see TWIN ice cream cones riding motorcycles! But even though these guys are twins, they have 31 differences. See if you can find them!

ON YOUR MARK
GET SET...
GO!

ROCKY ROADSTER

ROADY ROCKSTER

SECRET LANGUAGE CREATION CENTER

Hello.

I am your language consultant Mouse Horse. (That is my name in the language that I made up. Roughly translated to English, it would be Michaelannathorn Horseyganthia Petrellawellburtst, but that is a long name so we'll stick with the translation Mouse Horse.)

If you want to invent a secret language, first you'll need someone to speak it with you. Pick a person who is good at keeping secrets. Next, choose a notebook. Title it something like "General Documentation of a C@1109 Industrial Vacuum unit" or "Alton Township Water Usage 1990-92." This will discourage snoopers.

Today's technique is based on free association. Pick a word. (No bad words of course. Keep it clean, fellow language scholars.) Next, think about how that word relates to a different word. Then think about how that word relates to yet another word.

Here, I'll show you:

FRIEND = FRIENDSHIP = SHIP = BOAT = SAILING DURING THE DAY = DAY

I started with *friend* and ended with *day*. So, in our technique, *friend* now means *day*. Now, when I talk to my friend I say, "I really LOVE MY DAY!"

MY = MY STUFF = ME = STUFF THAT I LIKE = I LIKE THAT = THAT

So, now that last sentence is, "I really love THAT DAY!"

LOVE = HUGGING = HUGGING SOMEONE TILL YOU CRUSH THEM = CRUSH

And finally here is the completed sentence: "I really CRUSH THAT DAY!"

Then hug your friend so hard that she begs for air. Just kidding! (I had to add the "just kidding" part so you wouldn't sue me for crushing your day's bones.) Try to add ten words—and their associations— every day and practice, practice, PRACTICE! Next time we will explore a different approach that involves being able to pronounce words like:

ÐdʃoaᵭbℲeⱤilʒtℏer-rrrƐierrrrrrrrrr

Bye.

I'M HUNGRY, AND I ONLY HAVE TWO SANDWICHES! DRAW ME A FEW MORE HERE. KEEP IT TINY, PLEASE.

"SECRET LANGUAGE CREATION CENTER" BY MICHAELANNE PETRELLA
"DARE CORNER" BY GOODS EXECUTIVE STAFF
"TINY SANDWICHES" BY WALTER GREEN
"VISION QUEST" BY LAURIE KELLER
"HANGMAN" BY SHAWN HARRIS
"BELIEVE IT!" BY JON SCIESZKA

7

THE GOODS

SHARPEN YOUR EYEBALLS

LAST NIGHT

the family that lives underground snuck up into the candy shop and stole some treats. Can YOU find the twelve pieces of candy hidden in their secret lair?

HOW TO: AVOID A SHOWER OR BATH FOR AS LONG AS POSSIBLE, AND MAYBE EVEN LONGER

1. DON'T FIGHT IT: The key is *faking* this bath, and the more you protest beforehand, the more suspicion you'll arouse. When Mom suggests getting in the water, drop everything and *move it*. Give her a thumbs up. *Smile*, even!

2. LET IT FLOW: Too often, bath-dodgers forget to turn on the water. Big mistake, friend! That's the surest sign of *shower-fakery*. For realism, you'll have to "sacrifice" your arm. Place it under the water every 45 seconds for occasional splishy-splashy noises.

3. SINK, DON'T SWIM: It's impossible to get away with avoiding a shower without getting your hair a little wet and floral-scented. Plug the sink, run some water and mix in a hint of shampoo. Swirl it around and flick a little on your stinky head. Repeat until damp.

4. MOVE IT: If you were taking a *real* shower or bath, you probably wouldn't put the soap or shampoo in the exact same place you found it, would you? Answer: Probably not. Mix it up a little!

5. EMERGE: With a wet towel wrapped around your neck, say these words: "Wow, I feel refreshed! G'night!" Then get outta there before they figure you out. Scram!

REMEMBER THESE TIPS AND YOU'LL BE JUST FINE, **STINKY McGEE**!

*Hopefully, that isn't your real name.

PLEASE NOTE: UNCLE JON'S SCIENCE KORNER, NORMALLY SEEN IN THIS SPACE, HAS MOVED TO A CORNER, AND IS NOW CALLED UNCLE JON'S SCIENCE AREA.

THIS WEEK: MAKE YOUR OWN SUPERCOLLIDER

THE BURROW OWL LIVES IN A HOLE IN THE GROUND. HELP MOMMA OWL GET THE FOOD TO HER CHICKS! (THE DOORS WITH THE SAME SYMBOL ARE CONNECTED.) HURRY! THEY'RE HUNGRY!

UNCLE JON'S Krazy Fun SCIENCE AREA!

1. Dig a big round ditch in your backyard. 2. Line it with concrete and lead shielding. 3. Use a Cockcroft–Walton generator or other basic voltage multi-plier to accelerate particles to sufficient speeds to cause nuclear reactions. 4. Name the resulting particles after family & friends!

—U.J.

8

DISPOSABLE WISDOM BEARD

CLIP IT OUT. TAPE IT ON. WALK AROUND.

WHEN YOU ARE DONE BEING WISE, REMOVE AND DISCARD.

cloche hat

tea-time dress

sun hat

formal dress

dancing dress

fox stole

sailor dress

cut along the dotted lines

FLORA THE FLAPPER

head scarf

fur coat

everyday dress

a paper doll

We recommend pasting flora to a piece of cardboard.

brigettteb.blogspot.com

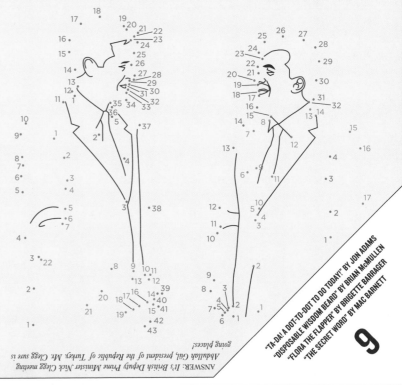

TA-DA! A DOT-TO-DOT TO DO TODAY!

Connect the correspondingly colored dots (sequentially) to reveal the exciting hidden picture! What do you think it is? Could it be a rocket? Maybe it's a monster! Perhaps your hard work will reveal the prettiest princess ever! Whatever it is, how can you rest until this mystery is solved?

ANSWER: It's British Deputy Prime Minister Nick Clegg meeting Abdullah Gül, president of the Republic of Turkey. Mr. Clegg sure is going places!

"TA-DA! A DOT-TO-DOT TO DO TODAY!" BY JON ADAMS
"DISPOSABLE WISDOM BEARD" BY BRIAN McMULLEN
"FLORA THE FLAPPER" BY BRIGETTE BARRAGER
"THE SECRET WORD" BY MAC BARNETT

THE SECRET WORD

We didn't want ordinary people to know the secret word, so we wrote it in the font Wingdings. Can you figure it out? (HINT: WE USED ONLY CAPITAL LETTERS.)

THE GOODS

10

Find Your Fate

Pick a Card
Find Your Fate

- Meet a saucy barber.
- Your dreams will come true in a minute.
- Do a lot of loud horsing around.
- Solve a mystery.
- Win a trip to Akron.
- Find true love at the market.
- Win a giant pile of quarters.
- Get a suit.
- Get married on a flawless boat.
- Hold hands with your neighbor.
- Meet a husky fella.
- Buy a homeless cat.
- Dig for gold.
- Give someone the stink eye.
- Meet a ragamuffin gal.

This Week's Periodic Table Quiz™

1. "Antimony" (**Sb**, atomic no. 51) translates to what?

- **A.** Against solitude
- **B.** Monk killer
- **C.** Difficult homework assignment
- **D.** Against mony

2. Cesium (**Cs**, atomic no. 55) is used by what?

- **A.** Mimes, to help them keep from talking
- **B.** Atomic clocks, for accuracy
- **C.** Scientists, to sound smart
- **D.** Dogs, to remember their names

3. The most abundant metal in the earth's crust is:

- **A.** Aluminum
- **B.** Carbon
- **C.** Aluminium
- **D.** Whatever they use in party balloons, door knobs, and aircraft carriers

ANSWER KEY: 1. A or B, depending. 2. B and C, but it would work for A. 3. A and D. Unless you're in the U.K. or Canada, then OK, fine, C.

CAN YOU FIND ALL 39 TRIANGLES?

ETIQUETTE CORNER

TODAY: The Most Fun You Can Have in a Nice Restaurant Without Getting in Trouble!

So you're going to a nice restaurant? Yuck. Lots of rules, lots of grown-ups, lots of weird things on the menu. What's a kid to do? PLENTY! Oodles of fun can be yours if you use this simple etiquette checklist:

✔ **You can't go under the table unless you drop something.**
So—drop something, pronto! (A spoon makes a good sound.) Once you're down there, breathe gently on people's ankles. They'll like that.

✔ **You can't throw things.** But you can knock over the saltshaker (by mistake—ahahahahaha) and spill some salt. If you do that, you have to throw the spilled salt over your left shoulder or you'll have bad luck. You can throw it pretty hard, too.

✔ **You can't sing at the table.** But you can hum! You can hum and hum and hum.

✔ **You can't play with your food.** But you can play with your napkin! Fold it into a triangle. Then roll up each side until they meet in the middle. Peel apart the highest point. Look! It's twins in a cradle! How great. (If this doesn't work out, make a napkin hat by tying knots in each corner of the napkin until it fits your head.)

✔ **You can't poke holes in your food with your fingers.** But you can make a face in your dinner roll using silverware. Gently dig your spoon into your roll. There. That's the smile. Put a single grain of pepper on the tip of the spoon and press into the roll. That's the eye. If you want a Cyclops, you're done. You can make a butter nose if you feel like it.

Have You Been Placed on Chair-Arrest? We can help! Put your hand on your stomach and walk quickly (don't run) toward the restroom. Clench your teeth together. Don't look sick—look determined. They probably won't stop you.

TODAY'S RED ALERT FOR BETTER LIVING: Sweetbreads are NOT sweet breads. They're brains.

DEAR EXPERT

Great question, Brianna S. It's a good thing you asked an expert. Here's what you do:

PREP: Try to get plenty of rest the night before. Between nine and 17 hours of sleep should do it.

ALLIANCE: Just like in life, it's important to have a pal who's looking out for you. Coordinate with a confidante, who will gently elbow you in the ribs if you're drifting off. You'll do the same for them. Teamwork!

DISCOMFORT: Bring your least favorite pajamas, preferably the pair with the tag that itches. And put a hairbrush in your pillow.

ACTION: Getting sleepy? Do 50 jumping jacks on the porch. What's your favorite awful music? Put it on! No matter what, keep talking. Remember the old phrase: "As long as you're talking, you're probably not asleep."

FINALLY: Never say, "I'm just going to rest for a little while." There is no "little while" in not sleeping!

Have fun being awake.

BIO: Jory John (actual name) is a self-proclaimed expert in most subjects.

GIVE YOUR FACE **WINGS** WITH THIS UNSCENTED PAPER MUSTACHE.

(CLIP OUT. TAPE ON.)

ARE YOUR PARENTS ALIENS?

IF YOUR "PARENTS" FAIL ANY OF THESE VERBAL TESTS, CONTACT THE U.S. GOVERNMENT IMMEDIATELY.

1. **ASK TO BORROW A MOP.** If they look up in surprise or blurt out "What for?" this is all the proof you need. Most earth parents know what a mop is and what it is used for.

2. **SAY, "MOM, YOUR SKIN IS LOOKING A LITTLE LOOSE IN PLACES."** If she displays anger or rushes off to examine herself in the mirror, what you are watching is an alien concerned that its human suit is malfunctioning.

3. **SAY, "DAD, WHAT'S THE LONGEST TRIP YOU'VE EVER BEEN ON?"** Telling the truth — over 27 billion miles — would give the alien away, so your "dad" will invent some earthbound journeys you've never even heard of. Push for details. Who was he with? Watch your "Mom" closely. Does she know about these trips?

4. **SAY, "I'VE HEARD THAT PRESIDENTS TASTE LIKE CHICKEN."** A human will respond, "That's ridiculous. No one has ever eaten a president." Any other response would be that of an alien worried about an information leak.

TSA IMAGING

FEATHERS LIE FLAT INSIDE SUIT

SNOUT COILS TO BECOME BELLY

THIS EXPLAINS WHY "DAD" CAMPS OUT IN THE BATHROOM FOR HOURS

TAIL FILLS ONE LEG OF HUMAN SUIT

ALIEN IN HUMAN SUIT

ALIEN IN ITS NATURAL STATE

OTHER THINGS TO LOOK FOR: Does "Dad" claim he was once good at sports but now has a bum knee? Think about it: How fast could you run in a human suit? Does "Mom" get mad when you barge into the bathroom? Chances are good she's more worried about her **IDENTITY** than her **MODESTY.**

Which instruments don't belong?

GUESS SOMEONE'S WEIGHT IN THREE QUESTIONS

1. Are those supposed to be pants or shorts?
2. Are you sweating?
3. How much do you weigh?

LEARN **magic** FROM AN ACTUAL UNICORN

I LOVE MAGIC!

LET'S DO SOME!

COVER YOUR EYES!

RIFFLE RIFFLE

OPEN THEM! TA-DA!

CUPCAKE RAIN

WEEEEEE! MAGIC!

Hi, reader. The eight words listed below are all misspelled on porpoise. Underline the one wrong letter in each word to reveal an excellent eight-letter word for a dolphin's blowhole.

BULLDOSER
BARPERSHOP
PINCIL
RURPLE
TENDERAZE
FANTACTIC
SPONGL
ERESER

I TAUGHT HIM THAT.

NUMBER GUESSING WITH GOAT

1. Pick a number between one and ten.
2. Nope, it was three.
3. Ta-da!

P.S. We've hidden this week's secret word to protect it from ordinary people. To see it, cut out the seven colored rectangles and arrange them in the order of a rainbow's colors.

G E B D I L D D U D

How to tell Fortunes

1. Be interesting.

Hmm.... this is very interesting.

2. Be exciting.

Wow! Amazing!

3. Be vague.

Your future is really great and fun-ish. Probably.

4. Be subtle.

You will pay me money for this fortune!

UNICORN, GOAT, BIRD, AND BEAR BY BOB SHEA & JARED CHAPMAN
"FIND THE MISSPELLINGS" BY BRIAN McMULLEN
"FIND THE SECRET WORD" BY MAC BARNETT

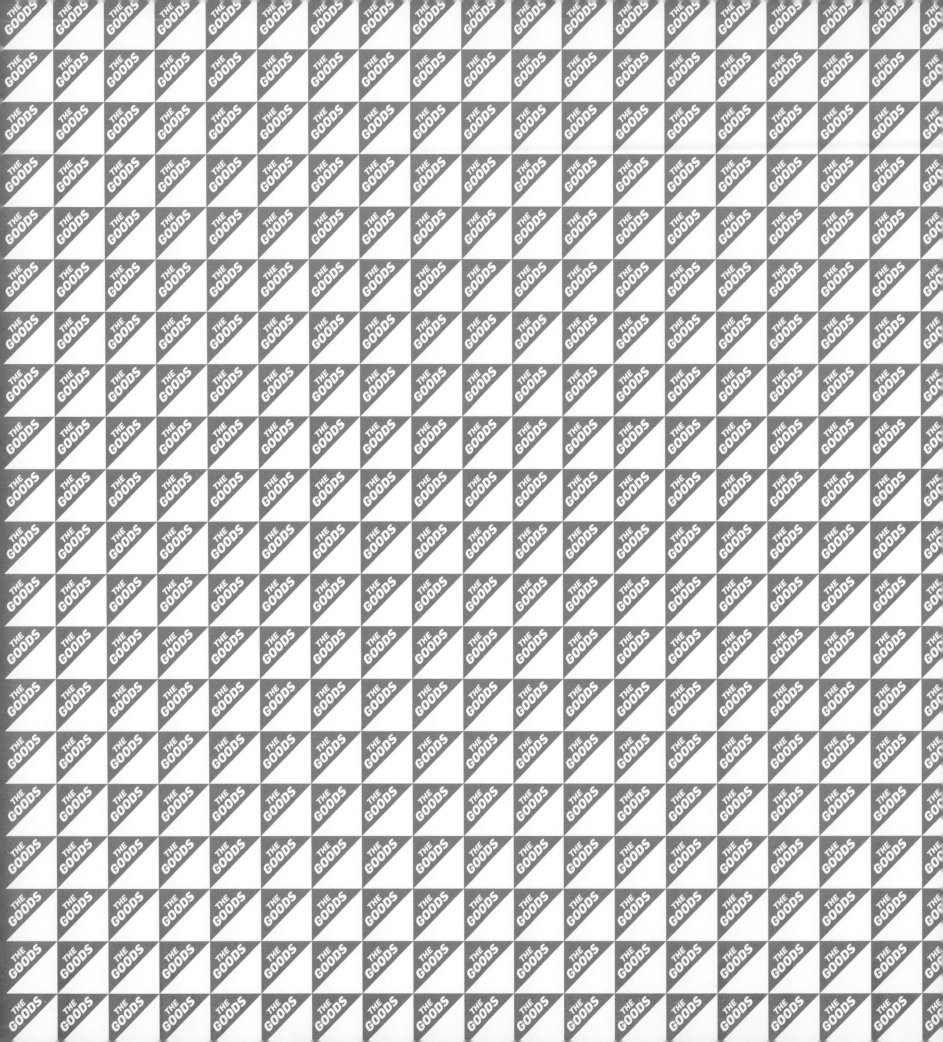

THE GOODS

ATTENTION KIDS WHO LIKE ART AND/OR SECRET MISSIONS:

WE WANT YOU FOR

OPERATION BUCKSKIN CADILLAC

YOUR ASSIGNMENT:

Please draw a picture of the things described by the 608th word of the 1948 book *My Father's Dragon*, written by Ruth Stiles Gannett and illustrated by Ruth Chrisman Gannett. (Do not count the names of chapters or the boring legal stuff in the front.) You may draw your picture below, or on a separate sheet of paper.

PICTURE-DRAWING AREA:

GOOD LUCK!

SHARPEN YOUR PEEPERS

EASY PEEPERS How many leaky cream-filled donuts are in this picture?
EXPERT PEEPERS How many donuts, total, are in this picture?
X-RAY PEEPERS How many jelly donuts are in this picture?

"OPERATION BUCKSKIN CADILLAC" BY GOODS EXECUTIVE STAFF
"ORGAN TRADING CARD" BY NICK VILLALON & AARON RENIER
"BAZOOKA SHELL PUZZLE" BY MATTHEW MYERS
"SHARPEN YOUR PEEPERS" BY SCOTT TEPLIN

13

ARE YOU A CONFORMIST?

A conformist is someone who acts and thinks like everyone else. This brief exam should clear up any doubts. **Do you…**

1. **Think kittens are cute?**
2. **Walk** *forward*?
3. **Consume food often (every 1–17 days)?**
4. **Think dolphins may be smart?**
5. **Brush your teeth** *after* **eating?**
6. **Recoil at the smell of rotting cattle?**
7. **Think war is sort of bad but sort of cool?**
8. **Ever look at newspapers?**

Count the number of times you answered "yes" to see if you are an independent thinker.

SCORING GUIDE — 7 or 8 yeses: We're surprised you could even take this test alone. **5 or 6 yeses:** You have a healthy suspicion of trends. **3 or 4 yeses:** Excellent! You have a strong will and are an independent thinker. **1 or 2 yeses:** What a maverick! Too bad you live alone. **Zero yeses:** Refer to our quiz, "Are You A Habitual Liar?" **Refused to take this dumb quiz?** You will be the leader of a revolution before your 30th birthday.

(QUIZ CODE: ALHBS)
(NOTE: ABOVE CODE MEANS NOTHING.)

Dinosaur Cut-Outs

Instructions: Cut out the characters along the dotted lines. Place glue or double-stick tape between the two pieces. Fold the bottom tab so that the characters can stand upright.

GREAT "THE GOODS" SCAVENGER HUNT

The word HOBBLEDEHOY is hidden somewhere on this page. See if you can find it!

HIGHLIGHTS FROM THE MARCH 2013 ISSUE OF

L.C.S.C.P.S. COCONAUT

THE OFFICIAL NEWSLETTER OF THE LUCAS COUNTY (OH) SOCIETY FOR COCONUT PUN STANDARDS

Two readers from Sylvania have now emailed to ask what we'd call a coconut that has begun to sound like a frog. Our best advice is to refer to all such coconuts as "croak-o-nuts." …… Rusty from Toledo writes: "I have here, in my hand, a coconut with a very large stomach. The stomach of the coconut is so large, in fact, that the coconut is just about to bust out of his little shirt. Could I safely refer to this coconut's stomach as his big old coco-gut? Let me know what you think." Rusty: We think yes. Whenever you find yourself needing to refer to a coconut's stomach— whether that stomach is large or small — you may safely refer to the coconut's stomach as its "coco-gut." …… Lifelong reader Pearl asks if it's okay to call a British coconut a "bloke-o-nut." Pearl: please stop asking us this question over and over and over. Yes.

—*Ed.*

THE GOODS

PINKY MANICURIOS, FINGER HABERDASHER

YOU SIMPLY **MUST** TRY ON MY EXQUISITE COLLECTION OF **FINGERHATS!**

CUT ALL THE WAY AROUND THE HAT.

FOLD IN HALF and CUT ALONG EACH DOTTED LINE.

DON'T CUT ALL THE WAY TO THE EDGE!

SLIP FINGER THROUGH

why not draw a face?

MA**SON**IC!

OOH, RUGGED.

AHOY, THERE!

OOM PAH **PAH!**

NOTICE:

As a public service, we provide new answers to old riddles—because there's nothing worse than telling a riddle to someone who already knows the answer.

THE RIDDLE:

A man is found dead in a room with 53 bicycles around him. What happened?

THE OLD ANSWER:

The man was cheating at cards. He was using a Bicycle-brand deck of cards—there should have been only 52 cards, but he had an extra ace. Someone got angry and killed him.

THE NEW ANSWER:

This story is pretty famous and I'm surprised you haven't heard it before. The dead man was Pierre LeFete, a Parisian who held many world records for eating strange objects. (Here are some things Monsieur LeFete ate: a set of steak knives, a jumbo jet, and a Peugeot 505 [a type of small but delicious car]). LeFete had an archrival, Jacques Dupont, a slightly less impressive extreme eater whose records had all been smashed by LeFete (Dupont's feats of eating: a spoon collection, a biplane, and a Peugeot 107 [an even smaller but also quite delicious car]).

On the day this story occurs, LeFete was prepared to once again outshine Dupont, this time by eating fifty-three bicycles (breaking the lesser man's record of 52 bicycles and one unicycle). But the scoundrel Dupont, driven mad by a string of public defeats, snuck into the exhibition hall early that morning and coated the bikes with a deadly, untraceable poison. LeFete had not even made it past the handlebar of his first Schwinn before he perished. It was a great tragedy in the extreme eating scene.

Luckily, Pierre LeFete's brother was Michel LeFete, the famous investigator, and through several impressive deeds of detection, Inspector LeFete was able to solve the crime and put the villainous Dupont in jail, where he remained for forty-five years, until one day he ate the iron bars to his cell and escaped, requiring Inspector LeFete to come out of retirement and apprehend the prisoner, which the great detective did with an amazing exploit involving a giant magnet. ◆

PARROT MASON'S Six Similarities!

Six things in these two panels are exactly the same, although some colors have been changed to disguise them.

Study the evidence and uncover the truth!

DO YOU HAVE ANYTHING TO ADD, FINGERHAM LINCOLN?

NO, I'M JUST KICKIN' IT.

VERY WELL.

ELEPHANT'S HAT, LION, "W" TO THE LEFT OF CLOWN, FLAGS WITH "X," LITTLE GIRL, LION TAMER'S HAT BUCKLE

| 1 | 2 | 3 | 4 | 5 | 6 | 7 | 8 | 9 | 10 | 11 | 12 |

4   3   2   1

IF YOU'RE AN ARCHITECT DESIGNING A HOSPITAL, DO NOT USE THIS

INACCURATE RULER

Double-edged to be twice as wrong, this clip-and-save paper ruler makes an ideal measuring device for optimists, pessimists, and anyone who is just plain sick of "inches" always being the same length all the time.

"NEW ANSWERS TO OLD RIDDLES" BY MAC BARNETT
"INACCURATE RULER" BY BRIAN McMULLEN
"PARROT MASON" BY AARON RENIER
"FINGERHATS" BY ADAM REX

15

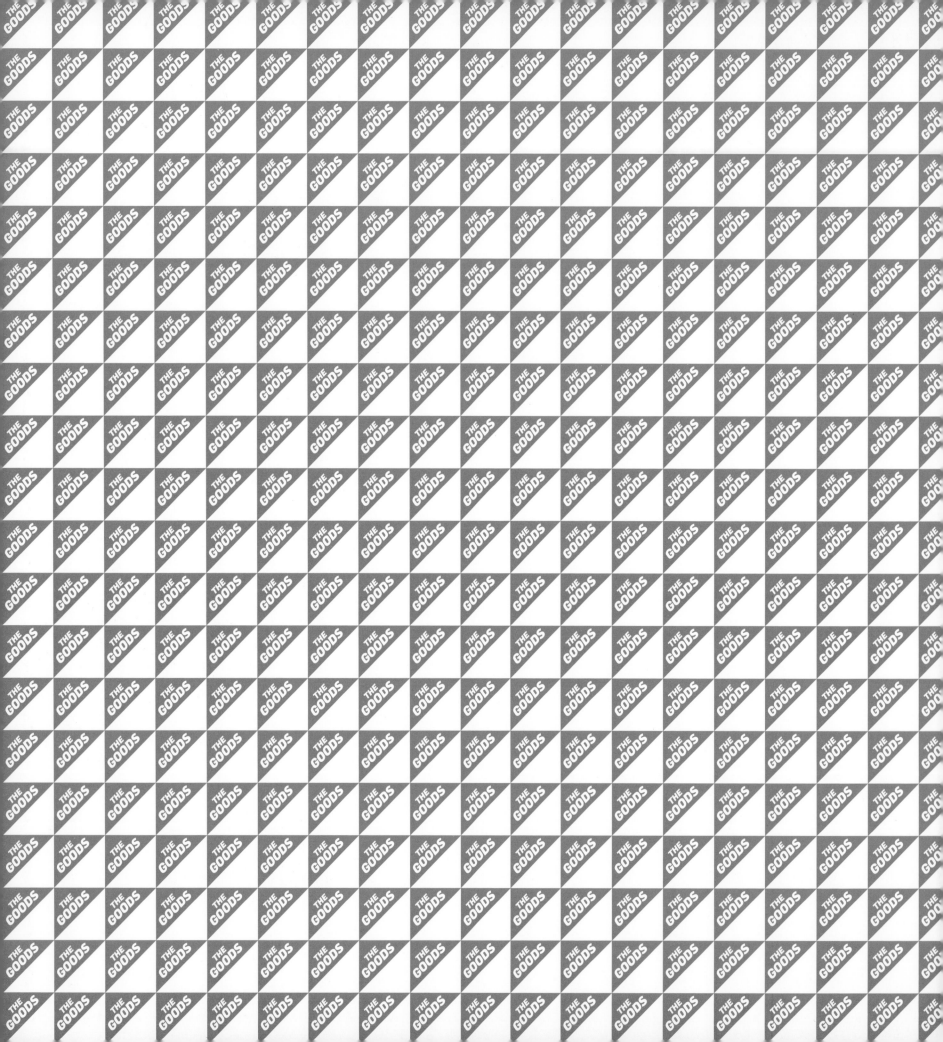

THE GOODS

WHO'S HOO?

CREATE YOUR OWN OWL!

1.____
2.____
3.____
4.____

A. BARN OWL
B. SNOWY OWL
C. GENERAL BLUE OWL
D. GREAT HORNED OWL

UNCLE JON'S KRAZY KORNER!

Myrmicology

Ants are amazing. Ants build their entire colony without using plans... or an architect. An ant the size of a human could lift a refrigerator and run a mile in 3 minutes. Ants communicate by tapping antennae and emitting smells.

BE AS AMAZING AS AN ANT!

1. Build a house without using plans... or an architect. 2. Fill your backpack with bricks and run a mile in 3 minutes. 3. Tell your friends and relatives knock-knock jokes by slapping them and emitting smells.

—U.J.

Ever wonder why the heck a hi-five is called a → hi-five ?!?

FACT: Originally called a Canadian-High-School-Five-Pin, before being shortened to the "Hi-five" we know today, the action of slapping hands in the air was a celebration that Canadian High School five-pin bowling teams would perform when a team-mate got a strike.

PSYCH!!! Of course you never wondered that!

But seriously, Did you ever wonder if cartoon characters call hi-fiving "hi-fouring"? also, if a human dude were to Hi-five a cartoon dude, would that be a Hi-Four or a Hi-Five?

One thing is certain... It would be fully awesome!!!!

Speaking of fully awesome, check out these NEW hi-fives all the cool kids are doing! the Turkey

take hi, poke low

the Snail antennae

AND the bionic arm! Simply transform your adamantium arm bone into a portal cannon, and launch an energy field at your friend.

THE SECRET WORD

TO PROTECT THIS WEEK'S SECRET WORD FROM **ORDINARY PEOPLE,** WE'VE PRINTED IT BACKWARD AND **VERY SMALL.** TO READ IT, YOU'LL NEED BOTH A MIRROR AND A MAGNIFYING GLASS: BUFFLEHEAD

"UNCLE JON'S MYRMICOLOGY KORNER" BY JON SCIESZKA
"SECRET WORD" BY GOODS EXECUTIVE STAFF
"WHO'S HOO?" BY CHRISTIAN ROBINSON
"HI-FIVE FACTS" BY SHAWN HARRIS

YOUR DAD *deserves* A MEDAL

Kid, take my word for it. It's true. He does. If you don't already realize it, you will one day, and you'll be happy you gave him this one here. You can still buy him a pair of socks, or a groovy tie, but give him this, too. He may get all gruff, and say that it's silly, but just about all dads are secret softies. He'll keep this thing in his wallet or on his desk forever. Count on it. Even if you're 37 and he's 62.

World's No 1 Dad!

THE SOLID GOLD "FATHER OF THE YEAR" STAR OF YEAR-ROUND PATERNAL EXCELLENCE

THIS IS FOR YOU, DAD!

WOW! THANK YOU!

They give medals for everything these days . . .

DID YOU GET A BIG ONE FOR CYNICISM THEN?

IMPOSTORS!

There are four completely imaginary creatures hiding among six real animals below. Can you figure out which beasts are real and which are fake?

BORNEAN FLAT-HEADED FROG

FLOWER-BACK BOX TURTLE

HELMETED HORNBILL

EMERALD-TUFTED PARM

TONKIN SNUB-NOSED MONKEY

BLACK-FACED SPOONBILL

VAN PELT'S FACE-EATING BAT

HAIRY-NOSED OTTER

DULLMAN'S GREY SPECKLED SWAMP SHREW

RUFOUS-BELLIED TREE BEAVER

VERy EXCITING GEOGRAPHY QUIZ

People in other countries say Americans don't know geography! (I'd tell you which countries but I don't know how to spell their names.) Prove these naysayers wrong by acing this **VERY EXCITING GEOGRAPHY QUIZ.** You can use a map if you need to, but try it without one.

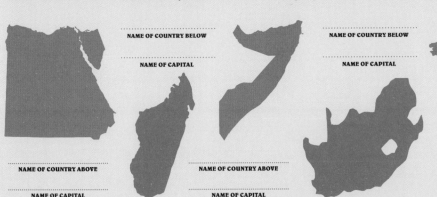

NAME OF COUNTRY BELOW

NAME OF CAPITAL

NAME OF COUNTRY BELOW

NAME OF CAPITAL

NAME OF COUNTRY ABOVE

NAME OF CAPITAL

NAME OF COUNTRY ABOVE

NAME OF CAPITAL

NAME OF COUNTRY ABOVE

NAME OF CAPITAL

1. **Four of these countries are in Africa. But one is in Europe. Cross that one out.**
2. **Write down the names of the four African countries.**
3. **Now name their capitals.**

Congratulations! You have earned America global respect by taking this **VERY EXCITING GEOGRAPHY QUIZ,** possibly while on summer vacation.

NOTE: COUNTRY SIZES ARE NOT TO SCALE. ANSWERS BELOW.

ANSWERS, LEFT TO RIGHT: EGYPT (CAPITAL CAIRO), MADAGASCAR (CAPITAL ANTANANARIVO), SOMALIA (CAPITAL MOGADISHU), SOUTH AFRICA (CAPITAL PRETORIA), FRANCE (CAPITAL IRRELEVANT. IF YOU GOT THIS ONE RIGHT, YOU CROSSED IT OUT.)

ANSWERS

The shrew, the parm, the bat, and the beaver are all impostors. The other six animals exist, but perhaps not for long—they are all threatened or endangered species.

"YOUR DAD DESERVES A MEDAL" BY STEFAN BUCHER
"FIND THE MISSPELLINGS" BY BRIAN McMULLEN
"GEOGRAPHY QUIZ" BY MAC BARNETT
"IMPOSTORS!" BY BRENDAN WENZEL

Hi, reader. The ten words listed below are all misspelled on purples. (Oops—I meant to say on purpose.) Anyway: Underline the one wrong letter in each word to spell a type of ship that is sometimes associated with the color purple.

JACKFT
RIEWPOINT
TABLIT
HAEDHEAD
CRNBABY
DONUD
SUNSSINE
ICHCLE
ENTRAICE
EGYPTIAN

The correct answer appears upside down below, along with instructions for this game's bonus round.

BONUS ROUND
Go back and substitute the correct letter for the wrong letter in each misspelled word. The ten correct letters will add up to a word that all purple objects and all purple friendships in this world are parts of.

ANSWER
A type of ship sometimes associated with the color purple is *friendship.* If friendship is not the answer you arrived at, then you have not played the game correctly. In this game—generally—friendship is probably the only worthwhile answer.

START AT OTHER END

WHAT KIND OF PARTY GURU ARE YOU??

WHEN PUTTING OUT THE FOOD FOR YOUR PARTY, YOU SHOULD BE SURE TO:

A) Make a slip-n-slide of creamed corn.

B) Put the glasses at the bottom of the punch bowl, add punch, and then have your guests "bob" for their cups.

C) Hollow out a watermelon and fill it with milk.

AFTER THE GUESTS ARRIVE, YOU:

A) Scream for 45 seconds straight as a way of getting everyone to go cah-ray-zay!

B) Have a roundtable discussion of your pets and their various ailments.

C) Turn on a home movie of you at your piano recital. The one where you throw up on the piano.

WHEN GUESTS ARE DANCING, YOU:

A) Show them your dance move called The Injured Lightning Bolt.

B) Turn off the music and have the chaperones rap battle each other.

C) Start a countdown. At the end of the countdown, just stand there looking confused.

MOSTLY A'S — You are a party legend!

MOSTLY B'S — You love a good do-it-yourself party!

MOSTLY C'S — Awkward might be your middle name, but hey, at least you had a party!

ONE OF EACH — You are the master of eclectic parties!

Did you know your eyeballs are basically natural soda fountains? And a big corporation doesn't own them — you do, so drink up!

JEFF KEMSKE'S LESSONS IN BODY SCIENCE TEACHES YOU HOW TO MAKE
TEAR JUICE

STEP 1

To begin, you're going to need to cry. Maybe you're kind of a wimp. For you, crying will be no problem. This will be your moment to shine. For those of you who are tough, crying will take some doing. Popular tear-inducing acts include: thinking of a departed loved one; embarrassing yourself; getting dumped; getting lost in the woods; rubbing freshly diced onions into your face; or contemplating life without the internet. Find what works best for you.

If you're just too tough to cry, or if there's a problem with your tear glands, you might also try harvesting the tears of an infant. Those things cry a lot.

STEP 2

Now that you've got your tears (you'll want about a pint), it's time to turn them into a beverage! Some people prefer straight tears, but I find them too salty. You're going to want to add things like sugar, lemon juice, or whatever you have that you think could improve the flavor. To be honest, tears don't taste all that great, but they're free and there's this kind of weird thrill you get when drinking them. Like you've conquered nature or something.

Then just pour yourself a nice, tall frothy glass and drink those tears away. That's all there is to it! Just two simple steps to create a drink that harnesses the power of teardrops!

If after your first sip you decide you aren't really into tear juice, why not send it to me? I'd hate to see all your hard, delicious work go to waste. I move around a lot and those jerks at the post office won't let me open my P.O. box ever since I asked a mailman to cry into a baggie for me, so email me at [email address deleted for reasons relating to tact —Ed.] for my current address. I'll reimburse you for the shipping costs. Or I can come to your house to pick up the juice directly if that's easier!

CAUTION: Because most states forbid (or at least frown upon) the sale of bodily fluids, this makes tear juice both rare and desired. Watch out for tear-juice addicts. They'll stop at nothing to drink your sadness.

Hi, reader. I've spelled a five-letter word that means "rugged and robust" by circling one letter in each row. Can you spell a five-letter word that could mean "thin and weak" by circling one letter in each row? (Note: there are two possible answers. Can you find them both? Look hard!)

Answers appear elsewhere on this page.

"WHAT KIND OF PARTY GURU ARE YOU?" BY MICHAELANNE PETRELLA
"ONE THING DOES NOT BELONG" BY SHAWN HARRIS
"HOW TO MAKE TEAR JUICE" BY JON ADAMS
"SPELLING GAME" BY BRIAN McMULLEN

18

SPELLING GAME ANSWERS: "WISPY" AND "FRAIL" ARE BOTH ACCEPTABLE.

Here is your chance to be a tattoo artist! Use a pencil or pen to draw tattoos on the circus performers.

TATTOO CIRCUS

Here are a few tattoo ideas you can use.

UNCLE JON'S
Science **KRAZY KORNER!**

MAKE YOUR OWN PREHISTORIC FOSSIL

1. Place a large, dead animal on the bottom of the ocean.

2. Wait 20 million years for mud to squash on top of it and turn everything to rock.

3. Dig up your own prehistoric fossil!

cut out the band members and tape them to your fingers

the hitchcock

the soul band

1. on with the lamp!

HAND SHADOWS
to impress and delight!

el chupacabra

trim out the onion domes and tape to...

↳ an iPod, phone, or cereal box flap. Also, wear OLIVES.

the taj mahal

trash and foliage

2 pens and a bowl.

who says hand-shadow fun is just for people?!

(spoiler alert) **the #1 dad** evil

the dutchess

the human handshake
(for dogs and rabbits)

2. off with the lights!

CONNECT THE WORDS

HOW TO PLAY: This puzzle is half word search, half connect-the-dots. To solve it, find & connect—in order—the words of the provided sentence.

FIND & CONNECT THESE WORDS TO REVEAL A PICTURE: "SOMETHING ABOUT THAT JULY FOURTH PARTY WAS REAL MESSED UP AND WRONG, DUDE."

DONUT WILL INK SANDWICH BOOT BUT BAKER MUSTARD A CAKE IS OUCH ABOUT PLANE GOLF RADIO SOAK OF MY NEWS PLANET FRONT RATIO ONE BOOK TAP TIE BRIGHT SUGAR EGG PLOP ANYHOW GRILL MOSQUITO WATER JULY THAT SOMETHING WORTHY UP COBBLER GOLD CHERRY CHOP CANE NEWT THANKS ABODE MATH AM TENDER DROP NOUN MESSED THAN GLOW WRONG HOUSEWORK MINUS FOURTH NORTH AT CRUMB PLATTER HARP GEL MY VERY GLASS GUYS WAS BELT LAD I BEARD PLUS BELL OILY BY PRO AHEAD IRRATIONAL RED DOOR NOW FAVORITE PARTY ROB REAL BREAD AND CEREAL UNTIL HAND MORE TIN UH POLAR SOY NOBODY'S DUSK DUDE FOE LAUGH RYE YES FLOUR GRIP SHATTER

COOK WITH YOUR FACE

Making food should be about eating, not washing dishes! Here's a recipe you can assemble in the best place to cook: your very own mouth. Who wants a mouthshake?

BANANA-NUT MOUTHSHAKE

- One (1) tablespoon milk
- One (1) one-inch slice of banana
- One (1) walnut
- One (1) small scoop vanilla ice cream
- One (1) spritz whipped cream

Shell walnut and chew meat until it is a paste. Reserve in cheek. Combine milk and banana in mouth, mushing them together with your tongue against the top. Reserve in other cheek. Scoop ice cream into mouth and let melt for 45 seconds. (If it is very frozen, breathe hard to help it melt.) Then shake head quickly back and forth, allowing walnut paste and banana/milk mixture to seep in from cheeks.

(NOTE: This can get VERY messy if spillage occurs, and it almost always does. Consider doing your shaking in a place that can be easily hosed down, such as a bathtub, an empty swimming pool, or a large municipal fountain.) Once everything is fully combined, spray whipped cream directly into mouth and enjoy!

COUNT THE STACK OF MONEY*

ANSWER: 4

THE CORRECT TOTAL is indicated by the ninth figure in the following list. Ignore the rest of the figures, which are all incorrect: $12.39 · $9.01 · $19.84 · $0.36 · $108.35 · $9.98 · $19.84 · $3.99 · $13.33 · $10.01 · $343.090 · $ N/A (trick question) · $10.03 · $2.99 · $1.00 · $3.35½ · $2,000.05 · $1,000,000,000.00 · $8.74 · $12.28 · $14.16 · $8.50 · $8.55 · $18.92 · $20.13

EVERYBODY STAYING IN THESE HIGH-RISES CAME TO THEIR WINDOWS TO SEE THE FAMOUS BOOK-READING BEAR. HOW MANY VACANT ROOMS CAN YOU FIND?

"COIN TOWER" (AND "MOUTHSHAKE" ART) BY SHAWN HARRIS
"GOODS CORRECTION" BY GOODS OMBUDSMAN
"COOK WITH YOUR FACE" BY JON KORN
"VACANCIES" BY MATTIAS ADOLFSSON

THE GOODS

We now present the world's largest-ever appearance, in print, of the word CLOPFRANT.

(Plus: As a free bonus for aficionados, we are also throwing in the world's second-, third-, fourth-, fifth-, and sixth-largest appearances of CLOPFRANT.)

CLOPFRANT
WORLD'S FIFTH-LARGEST CLOPFRANT

CLOPFRANT
WORLD'S SIXTH-LARGEST CLOPFRANT

CLOPFRANT
WORLD'S THIRD-LARGEST CLOPFRANT

CLOPFRANT
WORLD'S LARGEST CLOPFRANT

CLOPFRANT
WORLD'S FOURTH-LARGEST CLOPFRANT

CLOPFRANT
WORLD'S SECOND-LARGEST CLOPFRANT

ANIMAL   VEGETABLE   MINERAL.

19 HARD-TO-GUESS ANSWERS FOR "20 QUESTIONS"

WIN YOUR NEXT GAME OF "20 QUESTIONS" WITH THESE SUREFIRE STUMPERS:

A DUST BUNNY
MOSS
A GARAGE DOOR OPENER
A LASSO
A BREAD BOX
A SNORKEL
A SHUTTLECOCK
BINDER PAPER
LAUNDRY DETERGENT
A TREE STUMP
BIFOCALS
A PEPPER SHAKER
A CASHEW
A LADDER
SELTZER
A DIDGERIDOO
SMALLPOX
A TASMANIAN DEVIL
THE WIND

DR. LEEKY'S BEST and WORST DRESSED of the ANIMAL KINGDOM

From the the Himalayas to the Mariana Trench, animals are out and about this season in every sort of look. Who's the King of the Fashion Jungle? And whose style is extinct? Eminent zoologist Dr. Leeky weighs in.

LEEKY SEZ.... "The POLAR BEAR's coat provides excellent camouflage in its snowy habitat and features two layers to keep its body toasty, even when it's thirty-four below."

"But this all-white look just isn't slimming. What a natural disaster!"

LEEKY SEZ.... "I spotted this stunner near a hydrothermal vent off the coast of Easter Island. That wild fur isn't just for fun: it's home to colonies of bacteria that provide the YETI CRAB with nutrients."

"The only problem: since the yeti crab is blind, it can't see how fabulous it looks!"

LEEKY's Looky-Loo-at-you-you-you LOOK OF THE WEEK

"Wow! This South- and Central American stunner simply owns its colorful style, which comes from the high levels of poisonous alkaloids in its body. The enchanting hue also warns potential predators to step off—because the POISON DART FROG's toxic secretions can kill at a touch. That's deadly on the jungle floor and the dance floor!"

WHO WORE IT BETTER?

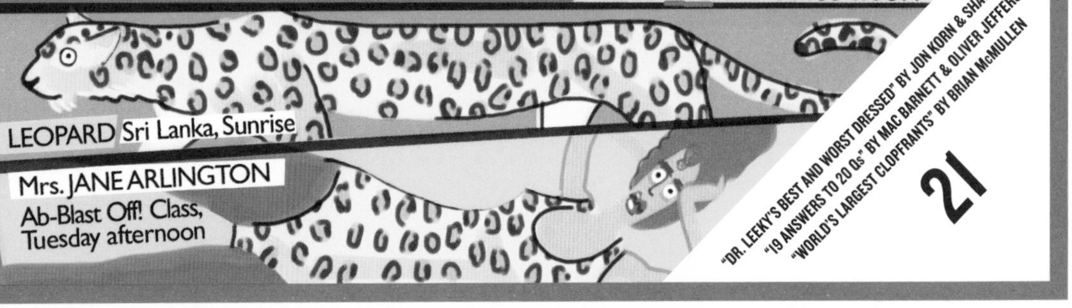

LEOPARD Sri Lanka, Sunrise

Mrs. JANE ARLINGTON
Ab-Blast Off! Class,
Tuesday afternoon

21

"DR. LEEKY'S BEST AND WORST DRESSED" BY JON KORN & SHAWN HARRIS
"19 ANSWERS TO 20 Qs" BY MAC BARNETT & OLIVER JEFFERS
"WORLD'S LARGEST CLOPFRANTS" BY BRIAN McMULLEN

CORGI MIX-UP

The queen has had over 143 corgis during her reign, which means it's high time for an upgraded model. Which of these new breeds does she have under development in her corgiboratory?

Corganary

We don't know what this is

Anteaterorgi

Porgi

Coraffe

Answer: Official statement from Buckingham Palace: "One must never mix such a thing." How dare you suggest lineage of traditional royal corgi!

ETIQUETTE CORNER
BY PRINCE HARRY

TODAY: How To Avoid An Unflattering Photograph At All Costs.

Hide. Behind a tree. Or a lady's well-appointed hat. Or a large and burly aide. A surreptitious sidestep is often all that's needed.

Create a diversion. Point and use an urgent tone to say something compelling such as, "Quick, is that man being accosted by badgers?" and make a run for it.

Employ camouflaging techniques. Bushes, twigs, and antlers can all be effective in this instance. The key is to stand as still as possible and think "stag, stag, stag" over in your head to give off an air of authenticity.

Blend in with the crowd. Just check the dress code and attire yourself accordingly. (Sounds simple, but be sure not to be led astray by outlandish fancy dress options in these instances. Ahem.)

And if all else fails and you can't avoid having your photograph taken, give them your best angle and smile. Just remember: always keep your clothes on.

What does one NOT carry in one's handbag?

A stamp: featuring moi

Parachute: for dropping in unexpectedly

Emergency pearls: essential back-up

A sword: for short-notice knightings

HAYLO

Royalty card: for I am royal…

Magazine: for checking the latest on one's family

A wallet: the contents of which bear my image

Ever wondered

what the Queen stows in her handbag? Here she takes us through the contents of her purse. All of these objects excepting ONE INTRUDER can be found in there. Can you spot the offending item?

Answer: One NEVER carries cash, so something as common as a wallet would not be found in one's handbag.

Kate's Cakes
VICTORIA SPONGE

William and I love a spot of tea and cake as much as the next royal.
Here is the recipe that helped snag me a prince.
Do try it yourself.

INGREDIENTS
1½ sticks/175g salted butter, at room temperature • ¾ c./175g white sugar • 3 large eggs, beaten
• ¾ c./175g self-rising flour • Raspberry jam & whipped cream to serve

DIRECTIONS
● Have one's cook (or other obliging adult) set the oven to 350°F. Then ask her to grease and line two 8-inch cake tins.

● Ask Cook to cut the butter into small pieces and place in a mixing bowl with the sugar. Have Cook beat them together, using a wooden spoon, until the mixture looks fluffy. Then request Cook gradually beat in the eggs one by one, and fold the flour into the mixture.

● Hand Cook a spatula, and have the mixture divided between the two tins. Smooth the tops of the cakes and bake on the center rack of the oven for 20-25 minutes. Now we're cooking with gas, as Grandmama would say!

● Allow the cakes to cool for 5 minutes in the tins, then remove and allow to sit on a cooling rack.

● Instruct Cook to whip the cream until it is firm, and spread on the underside of one of the cakes. Meanwhile, spread the top of the other cake with raspberry jam, and sandwich the two cakes together. Sprinkle the top with sugar. Yummikins.

Thank Cook and head off on your prince hunt!

Once I am Queen, this will be known by royal decree as Catherine Cake. Victoria has had it quite long enough.

"WHAT IS NOT IN ONE'S HANDBAG" BY PAUL COLLICUTT
"CORGI MIX-UP" BY SIMON BARTRAM
"ETIQUETTE CORNER" BY SIMON BARTRAM
"KATE'S CAKES" BY JENNY BROOM

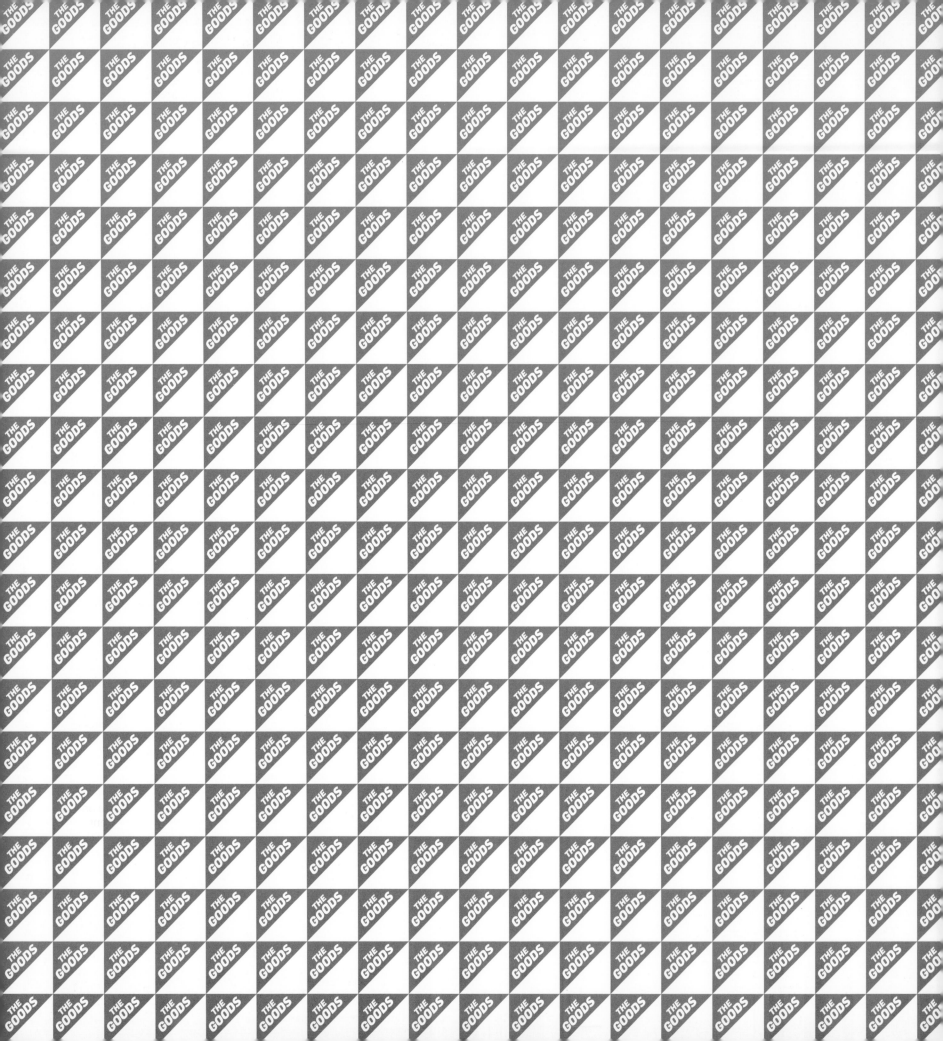

TOO MUCH LOVE

Oof! There's waaay too much love in this tiny corner. Help us take the first step toward resolving this problem by counting the number of extra humps on all these hearts.

The Bearskinrug

Bird Spotting Guide

THE DEFINITIVE VISUAL GUIDE TO YOUR FEATHERY NEIGHBORS, VOLUME ONE, NUMBER TWO, 1974

Birding changed my life and can change yours too...

BINOCULARS: A BIRDER'S BEST BUDDY

It wasn't so long ago that I found myself utterly incapable of identifying the various birds that were an important part of my landscape.

Luckily, this sad state of affairs didn't last. With only a little extra effort and heaping helping of education I was able to overcome my bird illiteracy, and my quality of life has vastly improved. Air smells fresher, food tastes better, and batteries last up to twenty times longer than before.

Sound good? It's not out of your reach! Grab life by the beak with this guide to the exciting hobby of Bird Spotting!

A.

Flying Bird

This is probably the bird you'll see the most often. The best place to find this guy is in the sky. Although once in a while you'll spot him on television or in the movies. No matter how hard you throw bread, he won't catch it.

B.

Blue Bird

This bird is blue. There's also a bird that's brown, and one that's red, and once in a while you'll see one that's white. As far as I know, there isn't a purple bird, so if that's what you're hoping to see, this is as close as you'll get.

C.

Talking Bird

This bird is always in the pet shop. No one wants to buy him because the people who work there teach him swear words for fun. You feel sorry for him, but just because you are an empathetic person doesn't mean you should spend $200 on a bird that will just insult your houseguests, right?

D.

Mad Bird

While looking out your window, you'll see this bird start fighting with a squirrel that got too close to its nest. At first you'll root for the bird, but after a while you'll start rooting for the squirrel because he has a fuzzy tail.

E.

Trash-Eating Bird

You'll see this bird in a trash can. At first you think he's gross, but then when you realize that he's choosing exactly the same food you'd choose, you're impressed. This is not to be confused with a bird eating out of a dumpster.

SPY BABY!

This baby is the world's greatest master of disguise.

DISGUISE THIS BABY!

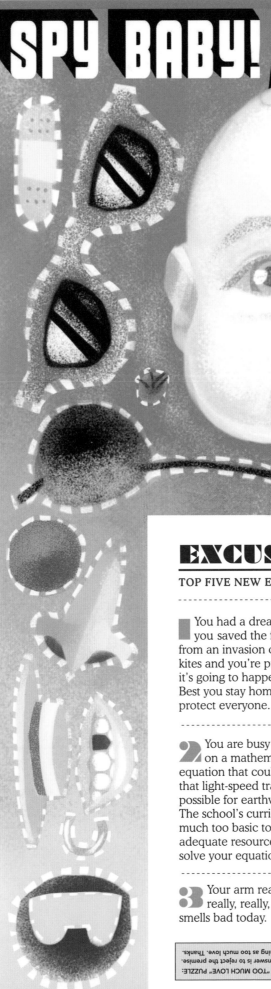

EXCUSES, EXCUSES!

TOP FIVE NEW EXCUSES TO STAY HOME FROM SCHOOL

1 You had a dream that you saved the family from an invasion of evil kites and you're pretty sure it's going to happen. Best you stay home to protect everyone.

2 You are busy working on a mathematical equation that could prove that light-speed travel is possible for earthworms. The school's curriculum is much too basic to provide adequate resources to solve your equation.

3 Your arm really, really, really, really, smells bad today.

4 You would go to school today, but it turns out that you are in a "waking coma" in which you can walk and talk, but cannot take spelling tests. You would like the school to send condolence cards to you.

5 Your hair may or may not catch on fire on the bus for no apparent reason. How bad would everyone feel if you were right about this? Pretty bad, you bet.

ANSWER TO THE "TOO MUCH LOVE" PUZZLE: The only correct answer is to reject the premise. There's no such thing as too much love. Thanks.

"TOO MUCH LOVE UP IN THIS PIECE" BY BRIAN McMULLEN
"EXCUSES, EXCUSES!" BY MICHAELANNE PETRELLA
"BIRD SPOTTING GUIDE" BY KEVIN CORNELL
"SPY BABY!" BY SHAWN HARRIS

THE GOODS

CONNECT THE WORDS

HOW TO PLAY: This puzzle is half word search, half connect-the-dots. To solve it, find & connect — in order — the words of the provided sentence.

FIND & CONNECT THESE WORDS TO REVEAL A PICTURE: "WHAT SHOULD THE WAITER BRING US NEXT, YOU DARLING DOGPANTS?"

BLINKER
TRUNK DAFT
CLUNKY SHALL
HALL
PUMPED DONUT
WILL
GRASP INK SANDWICH UP
CLASP BUT BAKER MUSTARD A WOLF HAM BRING US BLAST
CAKE IS OUCH ABOUT GOLFER PREACH JAUNT SHAM
GLOBBY SOAK OF PLANE
PRANK RADIO ONE GOLF ROLFING GLADDEN DROOP
DRANK RATIO SUGAR BOOK MY NEWS PLANET COP PRY MIRROR
MOSQUITO WATER EGG PLOP ANYHOW TAP WAITER TRY
GOLD JULY CHOP THAT SOMETHING BRIGHT GRILL CAMERA GONER
YO DOGPANTS DROP NOUN CANE NEWT WORTHY UP COBBLER DO DROOPY
WHAT HOUSEWORK MINUS THANKS ABODE MATH AM DUNGAREES
BANKER MY VERY FOURTH NORTH MESSED NEXT GLOW WRONG
BEES CLOUDY GLASS GUYS AT CRUMB PLATTER HARP GEL GOB
CHOMP TAMPER BY FAVORITE PRO WAS I BEARD PLUS OILY
DARK GOOFY TIES PARTY AHEAD IRRATIONAL BELT LAD RED DOOR BELL
CLAM FIN YOU REAL BREAD CEREAL NOW
TOOTHY COWER TERM THE HAND MORE AND PLUMP
CLING MOWER SOY NOBODY'S TIN UH DOUR GOO
TOWEL TONGUE FANG CRAYON TOWER FOE LAUGH RYE YES DUSK DUDE TEAK SOURS
DARLING GRIP TACK SHATTER KAYAK FLOUR ROLLERS YAK

"THE ROCK-PAPER-SCISSORS DOJO" BY JON KORN
"PAPER-WEIGHT TITLE BOUT" BY SHAWN HARRIS
"TEDIOUS WORD GAMES" BY BRIAN McMULLEN
"DEAR EXPERT" BY JORY JOHN

TODAY'S LESSON:
REVERSE PSYCHOLOGY

Tell your opponent which move you are going to use. Say, "This next one is Rock. I LOVE Rock." Your opponent will laugh. You will stay serious. Say, "Are you ready to Rock?" Check your watch and say, "It's Rock-o-clock!" Your opponent will be sure there's no way you're playing Rock. Then here is the thing: You do actually use Rock. This doesn't always work, but when it does, it always works.

MASTER CLASS:
PAPER VICTORY DANCE

There are three ways to celebrate a Paper win: 1) Karate chop. 2) "Walk Like An Egyptian" dance. 3) Turn your hand palm up and blow on it, like you've got magic dust in there that will put your opponent to sleep. Maybe even whisper "good-night."

THE
石頭
(rock)
紙
(paper)
剪刀
(scissors)
DOJO

DEAR EXPERT:
I'm starting at a new school in the fall. Any tips on becoming more popular than I was before?
—EVAN F., AGE 14

DEAR EXPERT

Hi Evan,
You've certainly come to the right expert! If I had a nickel for every time I started a new school in my life, I'd have 35 cents. But I could also just have gotten someone to loan me that money, because I was pretty popular.

1. DON'T WORRY ABOUT WHAT PEOPLE THINK. This is key. The more you worry, the less they'll think of you. Be yourself, unless, of course, being yourself means acting like somebody who really wants to be cool at a new school. Then, and only then, be somebody else.

2. BE JUST A LITTLE BIT DIFFERENT. Everybody wearing backwards baseball caps? Try turning your cap around so the bill faces forward, thereby blocking the sun. Everybody listening to terrible music? Try listening to music that's a little less terrible. Everybody wearing togas and fake beards? They are? Where do you go to school, Evan?

3. SAY YES. Quit saying no all the time. Take more risks. Get out of your comfort zone a little. Which leads me to No. 4…

4. GO BIG OR GO HOME. If you own a horse, and your school allows large animals, gallop into class on your first day. If that's not feasible, do something else, something amazing. Throw a party, a picnic, a concert, a gathering, an event of some sort. You'll be at the center of everything.

Have fun being popular, Evan!

BIO: Jory John (actual name) is a self-proclaimed expert in most subjects.

THE WORLD FINGER-BOXING FEDERATION
PRESENTS THE
PAPER-WEIGHT TITLE BOUT

CUT OUT BOXERS

AND FINGER HOLES

JAB WITH YOUR INDEX

BLOCK WITH YOUR MIDDLE

VS.

"STICKY FINGERS" LEONARD

"SUGAR" KANE GAROO

FIND THE WORD
THAT APPEARS EXACTLY THREE TIMES

HEAP TOAD COAT DOTE GO BOON BOB CLATTERING DOTE STOP SOUP AX
PANT THAT SOUP HAMBURGER SOAP COWL POLE SOAP BOLT ROAD STOP
COLT A GO DEEP BOLT THAT ROTE HEAP
DEEP COOP BRO TOAD SENSITIVITY ROTE PANT BRAT COAX COAT CLOD POLE MOPE LOOP BOOK COOP
LOOP ROAD MOPE COAX BRO COWL SOAP BOB BRAT AX

ROAD TRIP

If you've been driving around this summer, you've probably seen brown road signs, which mark areas of recreational or cultural interest. **But do you know what these actual signs mean?**

ANSWERS

1 Playground
2 Amphitheater
3 Spelunking
4 Kennel
5 Bear Viewing Area
6 Ferry
7 Rock Collecting
8 Environmental Study Area

IN **ALABAMA** IT IS **ILLEGAL** TO HAVE AN **ICE-CREAM CONE** IN YOUR **BACK POCKET** AT ANY TIME.

Given the following evidence, can you tell which suspect is GUILTY of this CRIME?!

• The wrestling bear buys two scoops of cookie dough in a waffle cone, daily. (Bear wrestling is prohibited in Alabama.)
• The culprit is not between 60 and 66 inches tall.
• In Alabama, it is unlawful to wear a mask in public.
• The culprit has previously been found guilty by the state of Alabama for playing dominoes on a Sunday.
• The shortest suspect does not wear pants.
• The culprit has not violated more than 2 Alabama laws.

...CAN YOU POINT THE FINGER

ANSWER TO "POINT THE FINGER": SUSPECT ONE.

---

344 QUESTIONS

THE AMBITIOUS STUDENT'S BACK-TO-SCHOOL GUIDE TO EDUCATIONAL GOALS, SOCIAL PROGRESS, AND PERSONAL FULFILLMENT

WHAT ARE THE TOP 5 THINGS YOU WANT TO ACHEIVE IN SCHOOL THIS YEAR?

IS ONE OF THEM "LEARN TO SPELL THE WORD **ACHIEVE**."?

"I before E except after C," REMEMBER?

WHAT CAN YOU DO TO MAKE THAT HAPPEN?

WHO ARE FIVE PEOPLE YOU WANT TO TALK TO THIS YEAR?

WHO ARE FIVE PEOPLE YOU **DON'T** WANT TO TALK TO THIS YEAR?

WHY?

HOW WOULD YOU RANK THEM IN ORDER OF CUTENESS?

WHAT WOULD BE FIVE **OTHER** WAYS OF RANKING THEM?

WOULD YOU RANK THEM IN ORDER OF CUTENESS?

IF SO, WOULD YOU ADMIT IT?

WHO MAKES YOU HAPPIEST?

WILL THEY WANT TO TALK TO YOU?

DOES THAT MATTER?

IS IT THE ONLY THING THAT MATTERS?

WHAT MAKES YOU HAPPIEST?

WILL YOU PLEDGE NEVER TO FORGET THE FOLLOWING?

IT'S **SHOULD'VE** OR **SHOULD HAVE**, NOT **SHOULD OF.**

YOU WRITE A LETTER ON **STATIONERY**. IF YOU'RE NOT MOVING FROM PLACE TO PLACE AS YOU'RE WRITING YOU ARE **STATIONARY**.

IT'S **DEFINITELY** NOT SPELLED **DEFINATELY**.

THERE IS A DIFFERENCE BETWEEN **THEIR, THERE,** AND **THEY'RE**. HONEST!

ARE YOU FAMILIAR WITH THE WORD PEDANTIC?

IS IT PEDANTIC TO CARE ABOUT USING LANGUAGE WELL?

IS IT PEDANTIC TO PRACTICE THE PIANO BEFORE YOU MAKE OTHER PEOPLE LISTEN TO YOU?

OR IS IT ACTUALLY PRETTY COOL?

ARE YOU FAMILAR WITH THE WORD NERD?

DO YOU CARE IF SOMEBODY CALLS YOU NAMES?

WHAT WORDS SCARE YOU THE MOST?

PERFIDY?

VICISSITUDE?

FATTY-FAT FAT FAT?

WHY?

WILL THAT MATTER IN A YEAR?

WILL IT MATTER IN **TEN** YEARS?

WHY DOES IT MATTER **TODAY?**

WHAT WOULD YOU WANT TO LEARN JUST BECAUSE YOU WANT TO KNOW MORE ABOUT IT?

WHAT WOULD YOU DO IF YOU DIDN'T HAVE TO WORRY ABOUT THE STUFF YOUR PARENTS WORRY ABOUT?

LIKE WHAT COLLEGE YOU'LL GET INTO.

ARE YOU WORKING AS HARD AS YOU CAN?

ARE YOU HAVING AS MUCH FUN AS YOU CAN?

WANNA SET A GOAL FOR BOTH ON THIS PIE CHART?

WORK TIME vs. FUN TIME

TIME PERMITTING

THE GOODS

VIVE L'EMPEREUR!

LONG LIVE THE EMPEREUR!

Guide Napoleon past the many obstacles and get him safely to Paris!

START

FINISH

NAPOLEON
The Emperor of the French

Napoleon Bonaparte was born in Corsica in 1769 and became Emperor of the French in 1804. The so-called "Napoleonic Wars" saw the French fighting many countries, including Britain, Russia and Prussia, represented in the maze by their national animals, the Lion, Bear and Black Eagle, respectively.

The small dog represents the pet of Napoleon's first wife, Josephine. The dog was named Fortunata (which means "lucky"), and he mauled Napoleon's ankle in the imperial bed.

Kittens may not seem a fierce adversary, unless of course you remember that the 5-foot-7-inch tall Napoleon, like Julius Caesar, suffered from ailurophobia, the fear of cats.

JACK PASSION
BEARD CHAMPION

Jack Passion is a Beard Champion.

He travels all over the world to compete in beard contests, where judges choose winners in categories like "Freestyle Mustaches" and "Full Beard Natural." *The Goods* wanted to know more.

THE GOODS: *When did you start growing your beard?*

JACK P: I started growing my beard in 2003.

TG: *What does your beard feel like?*

JP: It feels like wearing a scarf, a very soft scarf.

TG: *What kinds of thing does your beard get caught on?*

JP: Car windows, cat paws, babies' hands, helmets, zippers... The list goes on. I'm very careful, but some catches are unavoidable.

TG: *How big is your beard? How much does it weigh?*

JP: It's down to my waist, and it basically covers up my torso. I'm not sure how much it weighs, but probably not that much. After all, it's just hair.

TG: *What foods are best to help beards grow?*

JP: Nutritionally dense foods are the best. High-quality protein is a must, as well. My first law of facial hair is "healthy man, healthy beard." You are what you eat, and so is your beard. My beard diet consists of a lot of organic vegetables, beans, lentils, and grass-fed beef.

TG: *What does your beard do while you are sleeping?*

JP: I have to braid my beard up while I sleep. Otherwise I would get tangled up in it!

TG: *Does your beard have a name?*

JP: Some people call it "Big Red," but I've never given it a name myself. What would you name it?

Have you thoroughly surprised the face of somebody special today?

Why not do so—right now, or very soon—with our full-color, non-toxic...

Confetti Kit!

STEP 1 — Carefully cut out all confetti along dotted lines.
STEP 2 — Gather confetti into your favorite throwing hand. (Tip: Crumple it all up a little.)
STEP 3 — Find somebody you like or love, yell "I like you!" and throw confetti right in their face.

CAN YOU

MATCH THESE EYES TO THE ANIMALS THEY BELONG TO?

TIGER
HORSE
FISH
WHALE
LIZARD
PARROT

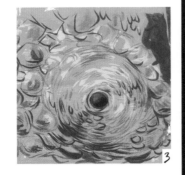

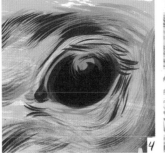 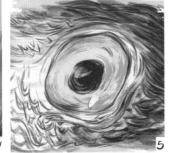

3 LIZARD   5 PARROT   1 TIGER   4 HORSE   2 WHALE   FISH

DETECTIVE SUGARTOOTH in the PREPOSTEROUS PANCAKE PROBLEM

A 3 PART IN 1 ADVENTURE

HOW THIS COMIC WORKS:

(GET READY TO FOLD!)

1. CUT OUT COMIC ALONG THE DOTTED LINE
2. READ IT. HUH? WHAT HAPPENS NEXT?
3. TO FIND OUT FOLD THE A LINES TO THE B LINES AND ALSO THE D LINES TO THE C LINES!
4. THE PLOT THICKENS LIKE PANCAKE BATTER! BUT WHAT HAPPENS NEXT? TO FIND OUT FOLD THE E LINES TO MEET THE F LINES!

MYSTERY SOLVED! ARE YOU HUNGRY LIKE A WOLF?

HELP!

This text is meant to be the <u>title</u> of the comic strip, but our writer has phoned in sick (from Fiji)!

fill in your own dialogue in spaces 2-4.

1. _____ (title)
2. _____
3. _____
4. _____

These two race cars came to the track looking almost identical! Can you spot ten differences? Huh? Can you?

VISION QUEST

WILDWOOD COYOTE ARMY
UNIFORMS & INSIGNIAS

205th Infantry Brigade WWD&BC* Patch

WW Army Flag of the Four

WW Army Officer's Badge

10th Sustainment Brigade Combat Service Identification Badge

Army of Belgian Occupation Medal

Drum Major

Silver Sun Combat Parachutist Badge

Private

Avian Principality Campaign Gallantry Badge

Order of the Red Dog

Officer

Commandant

Dot Dot Dot

Oustanding Achievement Ivy Badge

* Wildwood Drum & Bugle Corps

THE CASE OF THE MISSING BANANA/PHONE (age 8) by Audrey Young

I'm blind, I don't know if this is a phone or a banana.

Where's my banana? You took my BANANA! GIVE ME MY BANANA!!!

Just eat the phone.

"THE CASE OF THE MISSING BANANA/PHONE" BY SHAWN HARRIS (ART) AND AUDREY YOUNG, AGE 8 (WORDS)
"UNIFORMS AND INSIGNIAS" BY CARSON ELLIS & COLIN MELOY
"VISION QUEST" BY BRIAN BIGGS

28

THE GOODS

LEEKY SEZ... The **NUDIBRANCH**'s outrageous palette is proof that bright colors should be used in moderation - too bad these gaudy beasts can grow up to 24 inches long. These sea slugs use their poisonous appendages to keep predators at bay, but come on: who would want to be seen next to one of them?

WATUSI CATTLE

LEEKY SEZ: Fashion is all about making bold statements, and so are the **WATUSI CATTLE**. This big boy's groovy horns are even more humongous than you think, weighing up to 100 pounds! And don't miss that gorgeous dewlap (the skin fold under his chin): Now that's what this doctor calls really hanging loose!

Cheer-Ups

Sometimes everything can be stupid, mean, annoying, and just plain aggravating. Here are some ways to cheer yourself up.

Decorate the room for every holiday possible. Spend the day creating a multi-themed holiday experience in your bedroom. Combine Labor Day, Hanukkah, Halloween, Christmas, and Summer Vacation. Invite friends over for eggnog, lime wedges, and candy corn.

Invent a sport. Grab five things out of your toy box and create a sport. For example: Teddy-Bear Toss. Hula-Hoop Tennis. Baby-Doll Football. Building-Blocks Obstacle Course. Make a rulebook with a point system for keeping score. Test out your game until it's perfect.

Create a dramatic interpretation of your bad day with a musical play. Perform it for your family. You got a bad grade, then your best friend was rude, and you fell in front of the whole lunchroom. Take all that negativity and create a reenactment using made up songs, and end the musical with your transformation to a hero. Make it over-the-top dramatic and funny. Wear several costumes. Invite your siblings or parents to be props.

LEEKY's Looky-Loo-at-You-You-You LOOK OF THE WEEK

Animals care about two things: continuing their species and **FASHION**. Whose look is at the top of the food chain? ....And who are style's bottom feeders? Preeminent zoologist Dr. Leeky has the answers.....

DR. LEEKY'S BEST AND WORST DRESSED OF THE

THEY WASH THEIR HANDS BEFORE THEY EAT This **RACCOON** isn't worried about germs, but food feels better when his sensitive paws are wet!

ANIMALS - THEY'RE JUST LIKE US! THEY WEAR SUNSCREEN Not sure what SPF that mud is, but here's an **ELEPHANT** who won't get sunburned today!

LEEKY SEZ. Talk about a new spin on a timeless classic! Even though it's the most common bird in North America, I simply can't ignore the effortlessly chic style of the **RED-WINGED BLACKBIRD**. But only the gents sport that black coat with jaunty red epaulets and a yellow wing bar. The ladies are brown and white. Sounds like somebody needs a makeover!

Beauty and the Beast

Depending on how you look at it, the picture to the left is a portrait of a *beautiful girl* or a *hideous beast*.

SOLUTION TO THE SECRET WORD: "BANDICOOT."

THE WORD MINT

Some people make *paintings*. Others make *songs*. Here at the Word Mint, we make *words*. What does this page's new word mean? We don't know yet! Read it and come up with your own definition!

NEWLY MINTED WORD:

GRUYDAD

(THIS WORD IS #1 IN A CONTINUING SERIES OF NEWLY MINTED WORDS)

YOUR DEFINITION:

(Thank you!)

"BEAUTY AND THE BEAST" BY WESLEY ALLSBROOK
"DR. LEEKY" BY JON KORN & SHAWN HARRIS
"CHEER-UPS" BY MICHAELANNE PETRELLA
"THE WORD MINT" BY BRIAN McMULLEN

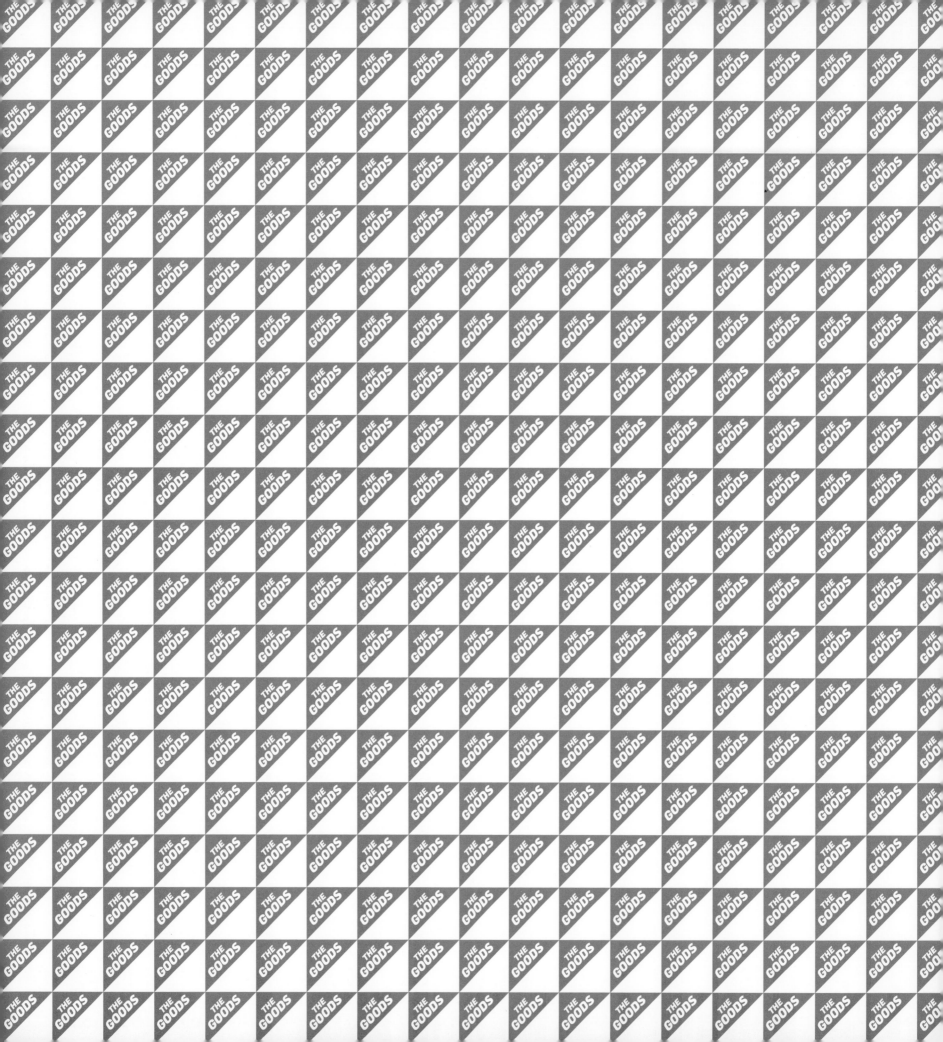

YOU CAN USE SEMAPHORE

TO SEND YOUR OWN [secret messages] sshh!

All you need is 2 giant flags! Or, if you'd like to avoid the notice of teachers and enemy spies, you could just draw pictures of little semaphore people and then discreetly pass -- a note.

What's the first First Lady's first name?

Which ice cream flavor is the best?

Can you come over for a slumber party?

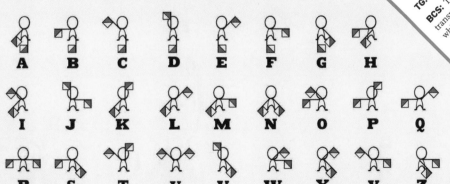

SEMAPHORE KEY

How did people send messages quickly before email or phone calls? In the 1790s, some crafty French chaps (the Chappe brothers) invented semaphore.* The Chappes did their signaling on dry land, but semaphore became a great way to say AHOY at sea. Isn't waving flags a lot more fun than swabbing the poop deck?

A B C D E F G H
I J K L M N O P Q
R S T U V W X Y Z

* Note: The brothers' original system didn't use flags. The flag part was figured out later, and the result is semaphore as we know it today.

BRIAN CRAWFORD SCOTT
CIRCUS RINGMASTER

Even though he never attended the circus as a child, Brian Crawford Scott became the 36th ringmaster in the 142-year history of Ringling Brothers and Barnum & Bailey Circus last September. As ringmaster, Scott is the most visible person in the circus, introducing acts, interacting with the performers, involving the audience and singing, dancing, and stage-managing. He spoke to *The Goods* shortly before heading onstage in Oakland.

THE GOODS: *How rigorous is your touring schedule?*

B. CRAWFORD SCOTT: Our work schedule is pretty heavy. We perform as many as twelve shows in a week, sometimes three in a day. We do between 400 and 500 shows in a year.

TG: *How do you travel?*

BCS: The train is our main mode of transportation. We live on that train, which is a pretty nice way to travel, actually seeing places in the country where the roads don't go. There's over 300 of us who travel together. It's like our own little city.

TG: *Who are your closest friends in the circus?*

BCS: I've made friends with some of our featured clowns from Russia. I'm good friends with the Human Fuse. I've got friends in the crew.

TG: *Who is the Human Fuse?*

BCS: He's my favorite act. He's lit on fire and shot out of a crossbow. I have the unique opportunity to be directly beneath

him when he's fired out of that crossbow. I see a man with a cape on fire, flying over me. And sometimes I can feel the heat from him.

TG: *Wait, if you have three shows in a day, he'll be lit on fire three times that day?*

BCS: Yep.

TG: *Is there any fear that you needed to get over to properly do this job?*

BCS: There's a float that we ride as part of the production number and the platform rises up in the air. I had to get comfortable with that whole heights thing. I'm singing the whole time up there.

TG: *How could a young person practice now to end up in the circus?*

BCS: It's all about being open to opportunity

and being open to the idea of being able to perform. And practice. If you want to be a juggler, you practice it every day. That's what the professional jugglers do. If you want to be a ringmaster, practice presentation and performance. It's all about being good with people.

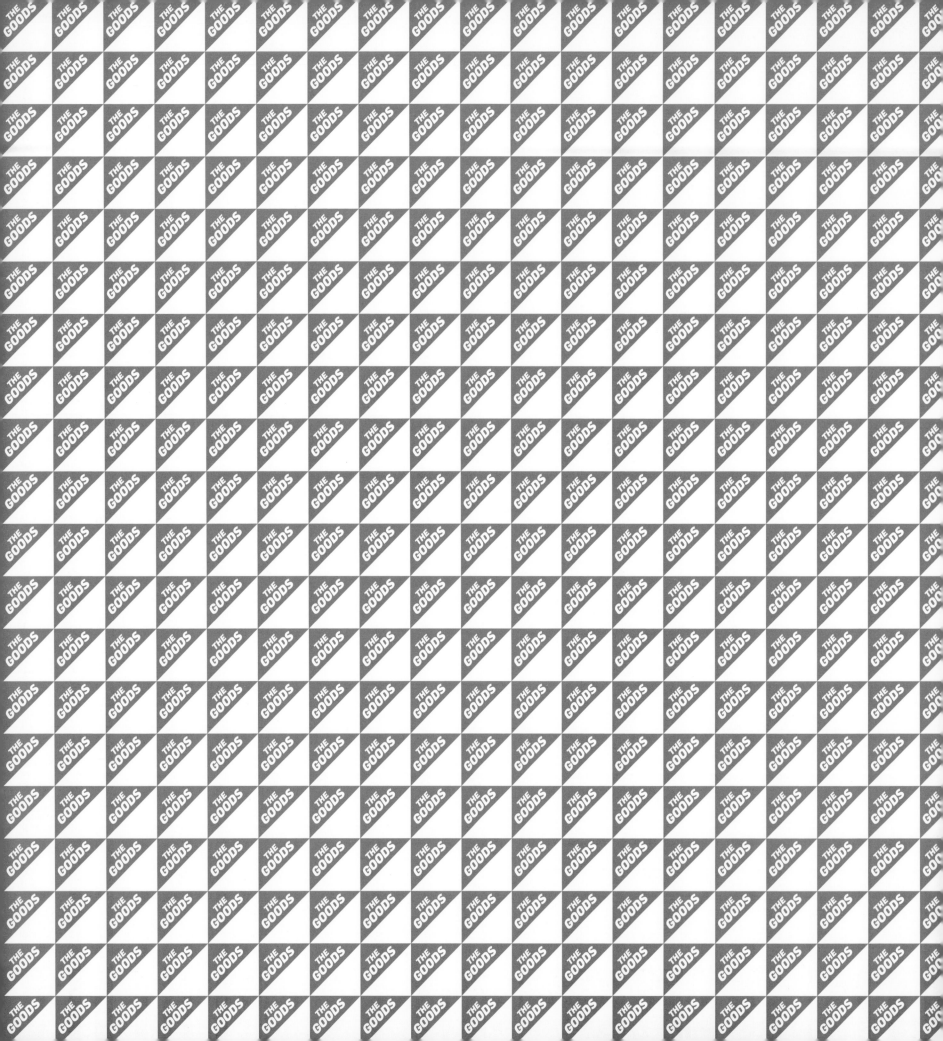

STARTLING

Can you find eight more words in the word below by crossing out one letter at a time?

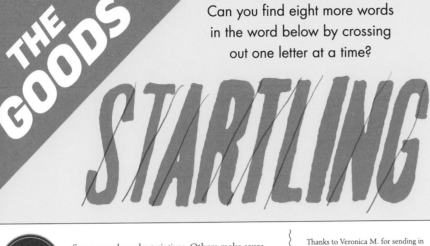

Some people make *paintings*. Others make *songs*. Here at the Word Mint, we make *words*. What does this page's new word mean? We don't know yet! Read it and come up with your own definition!

NEWLY MINTED WORD:

LARLON

YOUR DEFINITION:

Thanks to Veronica M. for sending in the rightest-seeming definition to the previous word:

JITSRISP

(N.)

ONE WHO IS COMMONLY ACKNOWLEDGED AS THE FOREMOST EXPERT IN A GIVEN FIELD

Veronica M.'s example sentence:
There are many talented actors, but Meryl Streep is the *jitsrisp* of our time.

"STARTLING" ANSWERS: 1. STARTLING 2. STARTLING 3. STARTING 4. STARING 5. STING 6. SING 7. SIN 8. IN 9. I

There is nothing weird

about an owl and a pussycat riding in a boat.

But there are thirteen strange things hidden in this scene. Can you find 'em and check 'em off?

☐ CANE/WALKING STICK
☐ CHEESE
☐ TELEPHONE

☐ CROWN
☐ HEART
☐ TOOTH
☐ SNAKE
☐ SPOON
☐ FRIED EGG
☐ LIGHTBULB
☐ GLASSES
☐ FISHBONES

☐ FORK

SPOT THE DIFFERENCES FIND ALL TWELVE

HOW DO THEY DO THAT?

DRAW YOUR OWN SHIP IN A BOTTLE!

DRAW!!

WHAT KIND OF BOAT DO YOU SEE?

"THERE IS NOTHING WEIRD" BY WESLEY ALLSBROOK
"SPOT THE DIFFERENCES" BY GREG PIZZOLI
"THE WORD MINT" BY BRIAN McMULLEN
"STARTLING" BY WALTER GREEN

THE GOODS

Here are the pieces to four exotic creatures:
an Iberian Lynx, a Great Hornbill, a Leatherback Sea Turtle, and a Siamese Crocodile. Cut them up and stick them back together just the way the way you think they were, or maybe make some new creatures. How 'bout an Iberimese Leatherbill? Or a Great Lynxodile?

EXTRA PARTS!!

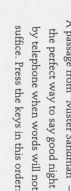

TELEPHONIC MUSIC

A lesson from
The Vienna Conservatory
of

A passage from "Mister Sandman" — the perfect way to say good night by telephone when words will not suffice. Press the keys in this order:

4	2	2
6	6	6
	2	6
		6

(Bravo!)

egg folks

Mr. Humpty ↗ (a plastic egg is best for this, but a hard-boiled egg would work too!)

1. cut out
2. wrap egg
3. (needs a little tape)
4. draw a face

Party hat ↗
(or dunce hat, for bad eggs)

Mrs. Humpty ↗

YOU'LL BE ONE SCARY PIRATE WHEN YOU
GIVE YOURSELF A BLACK EYE !!

DiscARRRd this piece. (It's where your eye goes.)

INSTRUCTIONS:
1) Cut along dotted lines.
2) Tape cut-out shape around your least loyal eye.

"GIVE YOURSELF A BLACK EYE!" BY BRIAN McMULLEN
TELEPHONIC MUSIC LESSON BY BRENDAN WENZEL
"ANIMAL PARTS" BY ALISTAIR COD
"EGG FOLKS" BY BRIGETTE BARRAGER

32

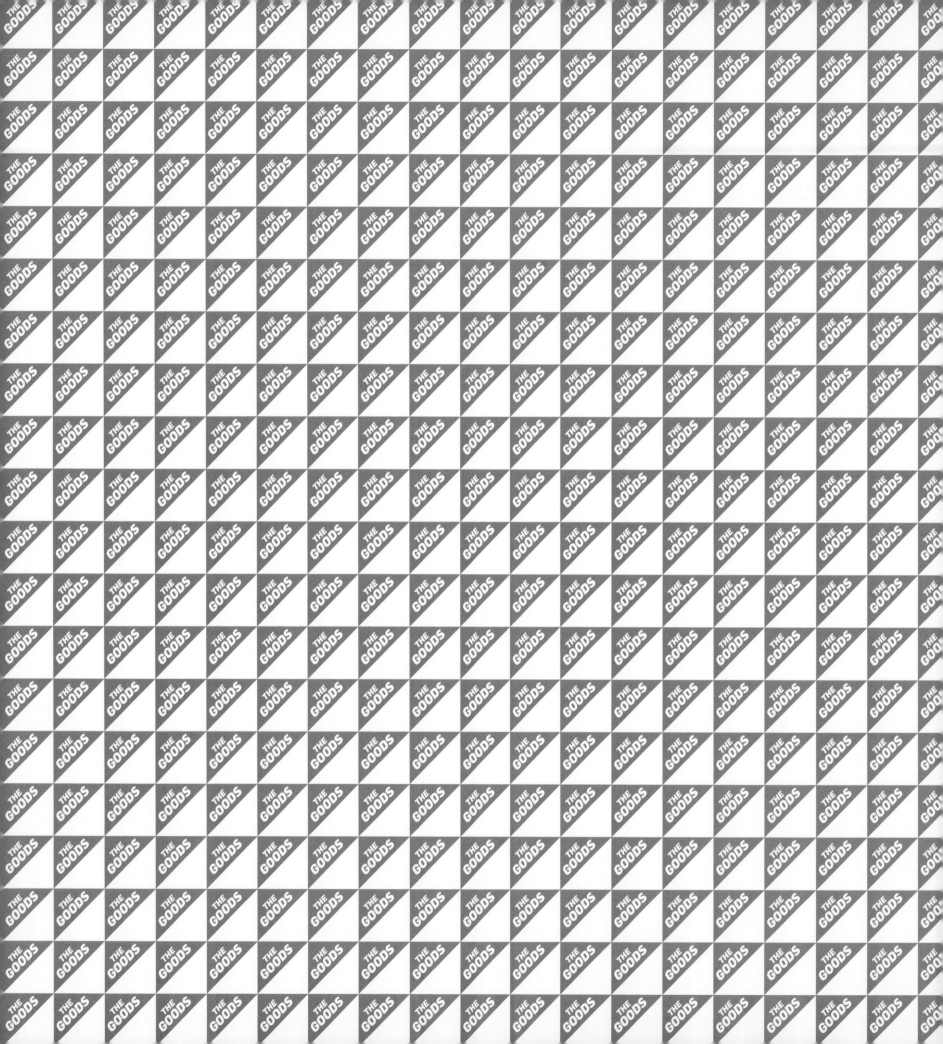

WIN A FREE BAR OF GOLD WHEN YOU SOLVE THE
FORT KNOX MYSTERY!

DEAR EXPERT: I'm tired of being broke all the time. Any tips on making money fast? Thanks!
—EMMA F., AGE 14

Fort Knox, home to the United States Bullion depository, contains 17 tons of gold but no outsiders have been allowed in since 1974. Just out of curiosity, can you form a plan to get in and out of Fort Knox with as much gold as you can carry and without getting captured or otherwise incapacitated? And can you send it to us before our rent is due?

HERE'S OUR FAILED PLAN. (WE GOT STUCK ON STEP 1.) CAN YOU DO BETTER?

1 BUILD TELEPORTATION MACHINE

2 TELEPORT INTO FORT KNOX

3 USE GOLD TO BRIBE WAY OUT

RULES: Mail your diagram-filled plan to The Goods Financial Department, c/o Sir Penniless Emptypockets, [THIS ORGANIZATION HAS BEEN SHUT DOWN BY THE U.S. FEDERAL GOV'T — SORRY.]. We'll test out the most promising plans and if yours works, you'll get a FREE BAR OF GOLD! If not, a winner will receive a very large gold-colored paperclip. Include your name, age, and address! Employees of Fort Knox and their family members are strongly encouraged to apply, as are all magicians, Ayn Rand enthusiasts, tank owners, and anybody with a solid understanding of the limitations of lasers.

DEAR EXPERT

Hey Emma,

When I was your age, I too was broke, but with plenty of entrepreneurial ambitions. And look how I turned out: I'm an expert in all subjects!

Here's what you do:

1. Let it be known that you need odd jobs. These don't actually have to be "odd," like balloon-folder, or anything. There are plenty of folks around your neighborhood who need a lawn mowed or a shrub trimmed or a hedge pruned or a door painted or a car washed or some leaves raked. And I'll tell you this: somebody your parents know is getting ready to take a vacation — right this second, in fact — and they absolutely need a 14-year-old to watch their pets. Their pets, Emma! And maybe you could even check on their house, from time to time. ADDITIONALLY: you could become somebody's personal organizer or dog-walker or babysitter. And so forth. Find a need and fill it.

2. Think about starting a business of your own. Starting your own business can certainly be lucrative. (Just ask Ben or Jerry of Ben & Jerry's. Those guys are rolling in dough. Cookie dough. Thank you.) ANYWAY, can you make/draw/write something neat? You can? Why didn't you say so? Go ahead and create that neat thing — say, a short story, or a drawing, or a bracelet, or a greeting card — and then sell it! If you have enough Internet-prowess, or know somebody who does, you could set up a website for your stuff. Or just sell it to your parents' friends. Whatever works.

3. Get rid of your stuff. Surely, you have toys that you're not using anymore, CDs (remember those?) that you're not playing, clothes that you've outgrown. I've got two words for you: "garage" and "sale." This weekend or next vacation or sometime soon, sell your stuff. People love garage sales, Emma. Give the people what they love, while they give you their money.

Have fun having cash, Emma!

BIO: Jory John (actual name) is a self-proclaimed expert in most subjects.

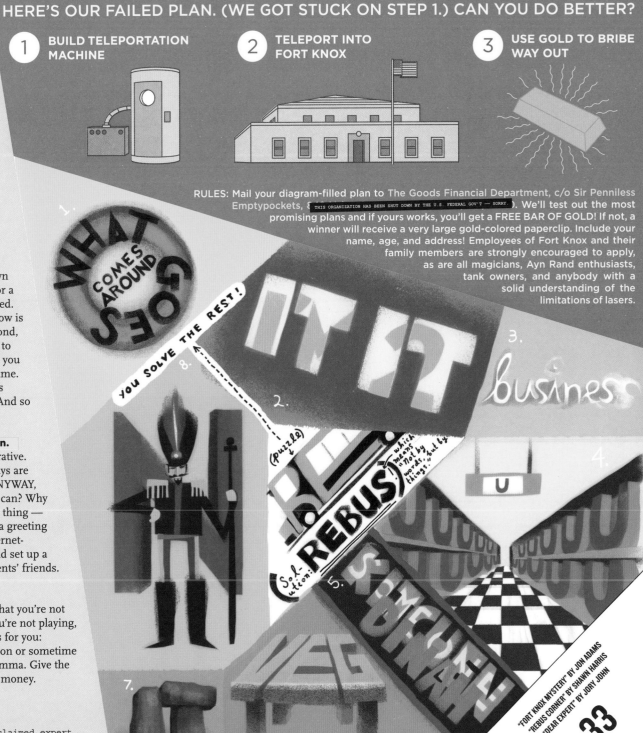

WHAT COMES AROUND GOES

IT IT

business

U

REBUS (puzzle) which means "not by words, but by things." Sol-ution:

SOMEONE IN DINAH!

VEG

YOU SOLVE THE REST!

"FORT KNOX MYSTERY" BY JON ADAMS
"REBUS CORNER" BY SHAWN HARRIS
"DEAR EXPERT" BY JORY JOHN

WOULD YOU LIKE TO PARTICIPATE IN A SURVEY?

☐ YES ☐ NO

THANK YOU FOR YOUR PARTICIPATION. YOUR INPUT WILL GO TOWARD A BETTER SURVEY.

Are you still reading the small print? ☐ yes ☐ no Actually, we can do away with these tick boxes. From here on out, just make some sort of mark on the page to signify that you are still participating. Are you still participating? _____ Was your mark a check, a star, an "x," or another sort of mark? Check, star, "x," or mark the box which applies.

☐ ✓ ☐ ☆
☐ "X" ☐ haphazard mark
☐ ▲ intentionally defined mark or shape other than check, star, "x," or haphazard mark

How great is/was your breakfast? Was/is it greater than or less (great) than the breakfast pictured here? Draw a little picture of your breakfast, or smudge a bit of it, on the appropriate side of this fairly average breakfast.

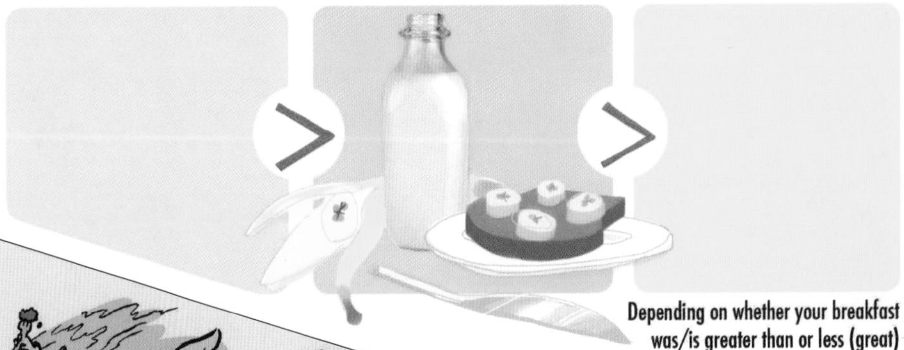

Depending on whether your breakfast was/is greater than or less (great) than fairly average, draw a breakfast which is greater than or less great than the pictured breakfast, in the remaining box.

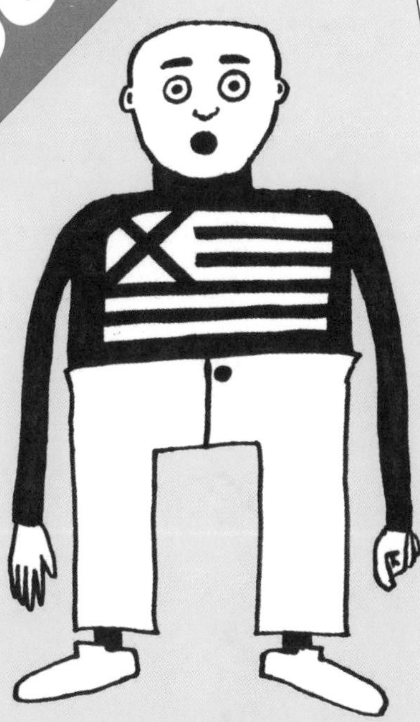

What country do you think this surprised man is from?

ANSWER: France.

THE WORD MINT

Some people make *paintings*. Others make *songs*. Here at the Word Mint, we make *words*. What does this page's new word mean? We don't know yet! Read it and come up with your own definition!

NEWLY MINTED WORD:

SWEFIDORY

YOUR DEFINITION:

Thanks to Neal K. for sending in the rightest-seeming definition for the previous word:

LARLON

(N.) A SPOTLESS, WELL-DRESSED CHILD

Neal K.'s example sentence:
The loving father doted upon his *larlon* at the annual blueberry pancake soiree, cleansing the child's cheeks and hands with a fresh paper napkin after every single bite.

A PICTOLOGOGRAPH

Each animal's name is an ANAGRAM, so if you unscramble the letters you'll discover the hidden word. After doing so bring down the letters in colored boxes to reveal the final secret animal.

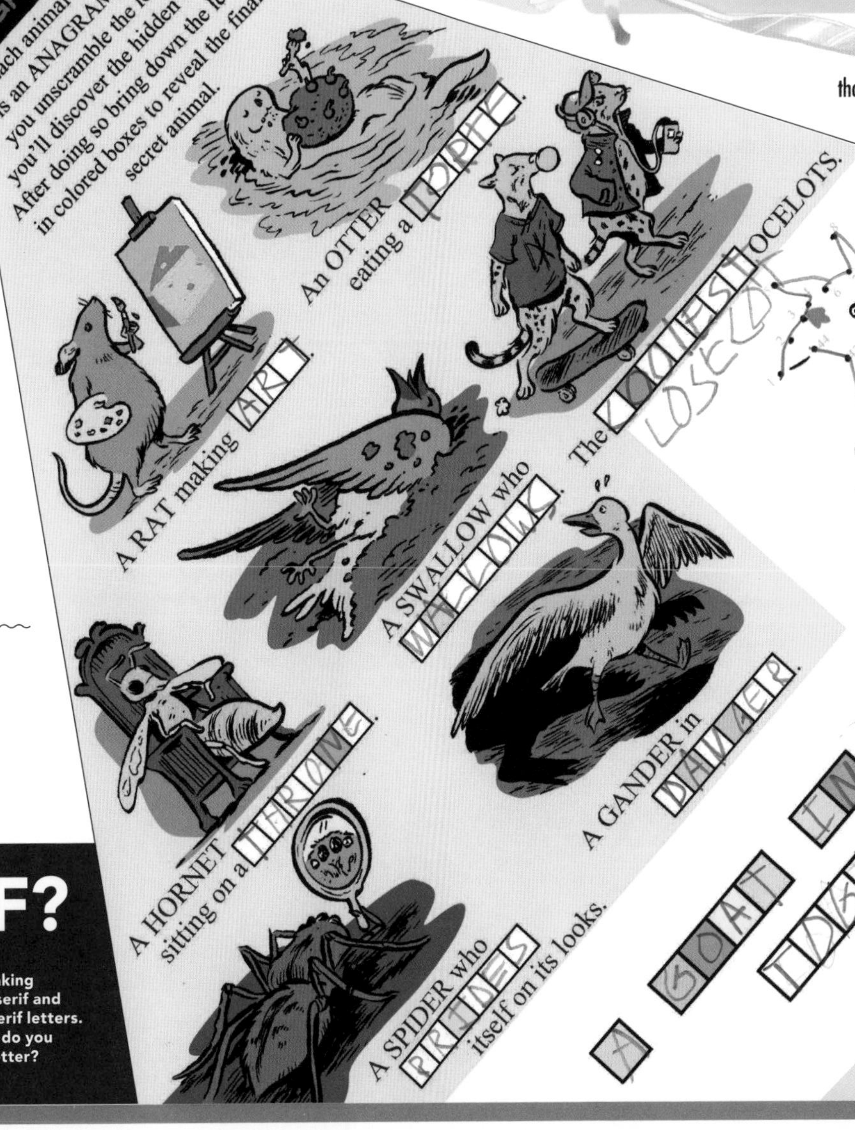

A RAT making ☐☐☐.

An OTTER eating a ☐☐☐☐☐.

The ☐☐☐☐☐☐☐ OCELOTS.

A SWALLOW who ☐☐☐☐☐☐☐.

A GANDER in ☐☐☐☐☐☐.

A HORNET sitting on a ☐☐☐☐☐☐.

A SPIDER who ☐☐☐☐☐☐ itself on its looks.

A ☐☐☐☐ IN A ☐☐☐☐☐

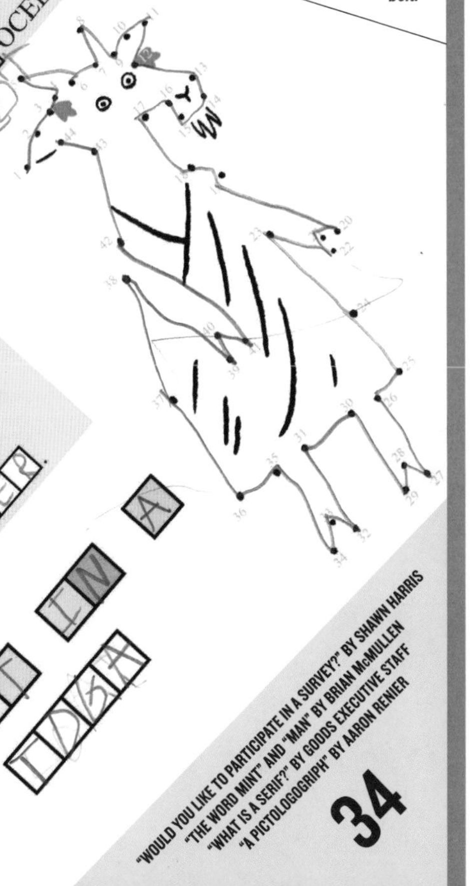

WHAT IS A SERIF?

Serifs are those little things that sometimes appear at the ends of letters: P

Letters that don't have serifs (like this one) are called "sans serif": P

Try making some serif and sans-serif letters. Which do you like better?

"WOULD YOU LIKE TO PARTICIPATE IN A SURVEY?" BY SHAWN HARRIS
"THE WORD MINT" AND "MAN" BY BRIAN MCMULLEN
"WHAT IS A SERIF?" BY GOODS EXECUTIVE STAFF
"A PICTOLOGOGRAPH" BY AARON RENIER

THE GOODS

WHAT IS IT?

a. triangle
b. piñata cone
c. pizza
d. party hat

a. strong man
b. giant
c. strong woman
d. horsey

a. real horse
b. seat
c. animal
d. drawing of a horse

a. seat
b. lion-taming device
c. kindling
d. Trojan horse

a. party hat
b. house
c. tent
d. triangle

a. lion tamer
b. superhero
c. animal
d. Olympic sprinter

answers: correct

A lesson from

The Vienna Conservatory
of
TELEPHONIC MUSIC

Fill the awkward silence in your next phone conversation with a touching rendition of "Mary Had a Little Lamb."

Press the keys in this order:

3	2	1	2	3	3	3
2	2	2	3	3	3	
3	2	1	2	3	3	3
3	2	2	3	2	1	

(Bravo!)

THE WORD MINT

Some people make *paintings*. Others make *songs*. Here at the Word Mint, we make *words*. What does this page's new word mean? We don't know yet! Read it and come up with your own definition!

NEWLY MINTED WORD:

DELNDY

YOUR DEFINITION:

Thanks to Beth L. for sending in the rightest-seeming definition to our previous word:

SWEFIDORY

(ADJ.) HAUGHTY AND CLUMSY; STRAINING FOR—AND LACKING—ELEGANCE

Beth L.'s example sentences:
(1.) I can't bear to read another word of this *swefidory* 800-page novel.
(2.) The groomsman looked sharp, but his toast was a bit *swefidory*.

Quick! Surround these angry guys with happy faces before they grow into a mob!

SPOT EIGHT DIFFERENCES

THE ANSWERS

1 SPOTS ON THE BUTTERFLY 2 COLOR OF THE FLOWER 3 DIAMOND 4 SHIRT BUTTONS 5 EYES (ONE WITH, ONE WITHOUT) 6 MUSTACHE (CIRCLE ONE LOOKING FORWARD, ONE LOOKING BACK) 7 SMILE VS. FROWN (ON THE SMALLEST GUARD) 8 HAT COLOR

"THE WORD MINT" AND "STOP THE MOB" BY BRIAN McMULLEN · "SPOT EIGHT DIFFERENCES" BY WESLEY ALLSBROOK · "LESSON" BY PROF. ERIK VON BÖHM-NEUKOMM · "WHAT IS IT" BY SHAWN HARRIS

35

THE GOODS

NUMBER

FACE

NUMBER

NUMBER

FIRST: draw a funky-shaped three-dollar bill in the space above. **NEXT:** clip it out and spend it on yourself.

Some people make *paintings*. Others make *songs*. Here at the Word Mint, we make *words*.
What does this page's new word mean? We don't know yet! Read it and come up with your own definition!

THE WORD MINT

NEWLY MINTED WORD:

ULYPRIKE

YOUR DEFINITION:

And thanks to Srikanth P. for sending in the rightest-seeming definition to our previous Word Mint word:

DELNDY

(ADJ.) WRAPPED IN STRING, ROPE, CHAINS, OR THE LIKE

Srikanth P.'s example sentences:
(1.) I'm sorry madam, the post office is no longer able to ship *delndy* parcels.
(2.) The *delndy* prisoners have no hope of escaping, although they'd really really like to.
(3.) The actor playing Marley's Ghost looked as *delndy* as a mummy. He had a hard time walking.

To farsighted **MR. CLOUD,** everything near just looks like squiggles and shapes. Grab a pen and help him recognize his spilled stuff by turning the **PINK SHAPES** into his belongings, and the **GREEN ONES** into rubbish. Also, you should probably draw him some clothes.

SOME COLORS HAVE WEIRD NAMES.

Can you match up each color's **NAME** to the **COLOR ITSELF?**

FUCHSIA
GAMBOGE
TAUPE
MAUVE
CRIMSON
VERDIGRIS
ZAFFRE
PUCE

DRAW YOUR OWN THRILLING SPACE ADVENTURE

	1.	2.	3.	4.	5.	6.	7.
SPACESHIP							
ROBOT							
SCARY ALIEN							
PLANET	1.	2.	3.				

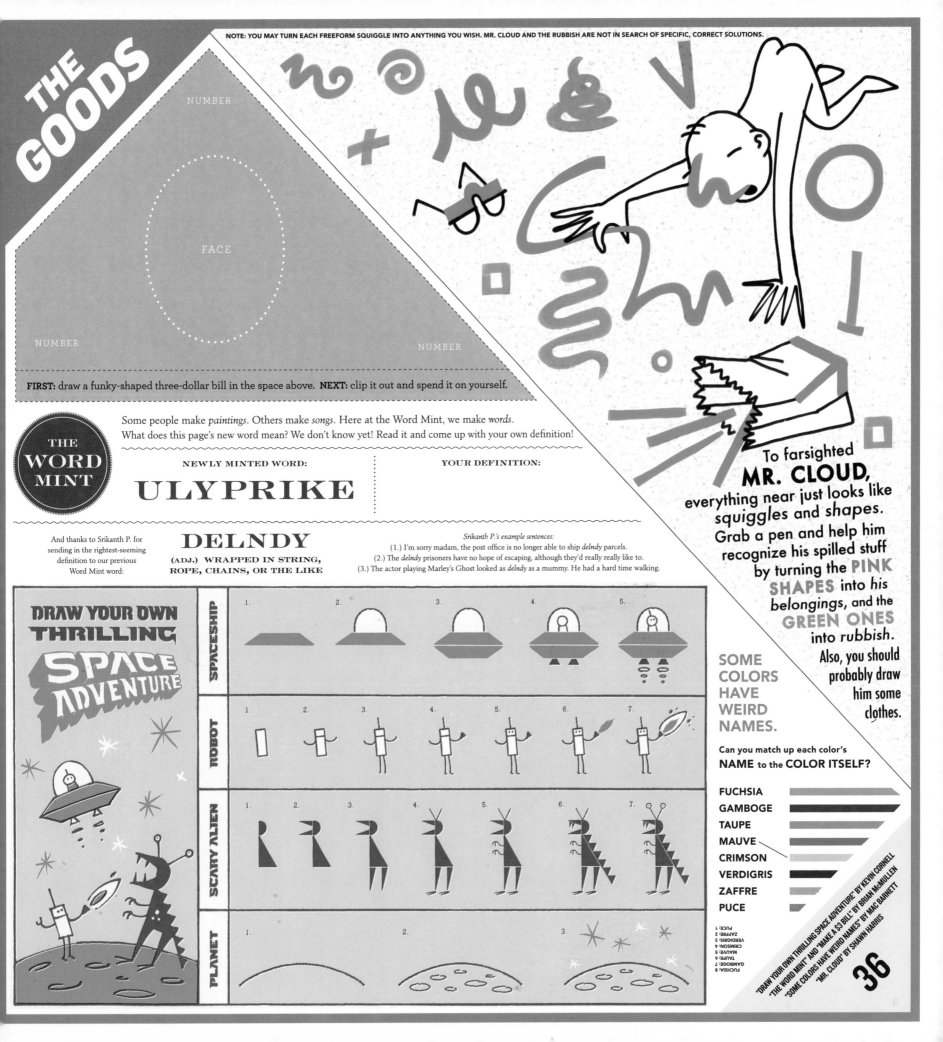

36

THE GOODS

OUCH TREY!!!

Trey accidentally told his twin brother Troy three tiny fibs, and now everybody feels a little terrible. (That's how it goes with tiny fibs.)

WHAT ELSE DID TREY TELL TROY?

I'll take very good care of your hamster while you're away.

FIND THE WORD
THAT APPEARS EXACTLY FIVE TIMES

MILK THORN CRUMB BULKY GNAW GLOOM THORN BULKY TO TRUE GLOOM GRIP TRAP THUMB WHO CRUMB DUE CLUB BROOM
BROOM DUE BROOM DUE THUMB MILK BROOM CRUMB GO TRIP CROP SHOP THUMB BULKY BROOM DUE BROOM BULKY THUMB
TRUE CRUMB THORN GLOOM THORN BULKY THORN CLAM CLUB BULKY THORN GNAW TRUE SOW CLUB THORN THORN
GLOOM CLUB TO
JOWLS TALE PALLET NICE SCOOP HOWLS SNOB SNOB
KNOB LIGHT MICE AD BULKY
SCOOP HOWLS WALLET NURSE NOR AD MOUSE ROUSE PALLET KNOB NOR CRUMB
MOUSE NOR NICE JOWLS

LITTLE MEN AND LITTLE WOMEN

We found the picture below on a page for "Little Men and Little Women" in the December 20, 1903 issue of the *New York Tribune*. We like it a lot, but have no idea what it means. Perhaps there's a good 350-word story to be written about what's happening here??? Are you up to the task?

A DREAM OF CHRISTMAS NIGHT.

THE WORD MINT

Some people make *paintings*. Others make *songs*. Here at the Word Mint, we make *words*. What does this page's new word mean? We don't know yet! Read it and come up with your own definition!

NEWLY MINTED WORD:

BEMPIS

YOUR DEFINITION:

Thanks to Melanie W. for sending in the rightest-seeming definition to the previous word:

ULYPRIKE

(N.) THE AREA OVER THE DOORWAY INTO A CHURCH OR ANY SACRED PLACE

Melanie W.'s example sentences:

(1.) A carving of an owl stared down at me from the *ulyprike* as I entered Athena's ancient chapel.

(2.) Although most of the building had crumbled into ruins, the *ulyprike* remained untouched by time, as fresh as the day it was carved.

(3.) My near-sighted local guide developed a rather nasty bruise on the forehead after he misjudged the height of the *ulyprike*.

WHICH WORD APPEARS EXACTLY FIVE TIMES?
THE CORRECT ANSWER TO THE "FIND THE WORD" PUZZLE ABOVE IS A FIVE-LETTER WORD THAT STARTS WITH A LETTER BETWEEN "B" AND "P" AND ALMOST RHYMES WITH "YOUNG."

SAUSAGE SCRAMBLE

Please unscramble the names of these sausages.

1. **UTABSRTWR**
2. **ORCN OGD**
3. **MISLAA**
4. **LABIAKSE**
5. **LRWTUVSEIR**
6. **ROOHZCI**
7. **AKENRFFUTRR**
8. **OOLNBAG**

37

Heh!

Hee!

Ho!

Ha!

My laughing face contains at least six tiny faces.

Can you spot them?

❖ HOLY QUEST MAZE ❖

HELP THE KNIGHT FIND HIS WAY TO THE ALL-SEEING EYE

START

THE SECRET WORD IS "WHISKERS."

THE WORD MINT

Some people make *paintings*. Others make *songs*. Here at the Word Mint, we make *words*. What does this page's new word mean? We don't know yet! Read it and come up with your own definition!

NEWLY MINTED WORD:

GURJUR

YOUR DEFINITION:

Thanks to Rachel K. for sending in the rightest-seeming definition to the previous word:

BEMPIS

(ADJ.)
PLEASURABLE TO LEAN AGAINST

Rachel K.'s example sentence:

Rosie selected a *bempis* tree to sit and read beneath.

WHAT DID THE DAIRY FARMER CAMEL SAY TO THE ARTIST CAMEL?

DRAW MY DAIRY.

OK.

Q: Where does a milk camel go to study theatre?

A: Drama Dairy.

WHAT DID THE DAIRY FARMER CAMEL SAY TO THE ARTIST CAMEL?

DRAW MY DAIRY.

OK.

Dear Reader,
Here (above) are two illustrated jokes about camels. One of the jokes appears twice for the same reason that humps appear twice on the backs of many camels.

THE WORD MINT

Some people make *paintings*. Others make *songs*. Here at the Word Mint, we make *words*. What does this page's new word mean? We don't know yet! Read it and come up with your own definition!

NEWLY MINTED WORD:

DARZE

YOUR DEFINITION:

Claw

SPOT THE DIFFERENCES

THESE TWO LIGHTHOUSE STATIONS ARE MIRROR IMAGES OF EACH OTHER, EXCEPT FOR TWELVE DIFFERENCES.

CAN YOU SPOT THE DIFFERENCES?

FIND THE WORD
THAT APPEARS EXACTLY FOUR TIMES

SAW SLAW ~~GNAW~~ ~~OH~~ HOT SLAW PINES   SHOW DART ~~CRAW~~ SAW DART LINES   BOP ~~OUTLAW~~ CLAW ~~GNAW~~
JAW ~~CRAW~~ SNOW ~~GNAW~~ CLAW SLAW ~~CRAW~~ ~~GNAW~~   ~~SLAW~~ AHA ~~OH~~ PINE   ~~SLAW~~ ~~JAW~~ CLAW ~~OH~~ ~~SLAW~~
~~OUTLAW~~ ~~CRAW~~ SLAW ~~OH~~ ~~SAW~~ AHA ~~GNAW~~ ~~CRAW~~   ~~OH~~ SPINE GNAW ~~OUTLAW~~ MILD ~~OH~~ CLAW ~~SLAW~~ SAW ~~GNAW~~ ~~JAW~~ SLAW ~~SAW~~ JAW

HOW TO FAKE A HORRIBLE FAKE ILLNESS

THERE ARE LOTS OF REASONS TO FAKE A HORRIBLE FAKE ILLNESS (SPELLING TEST, ORGAN MEATS FOR DINNER, HAVING TO RUN IN P.E., OR PEOPLE SIMPLY FORGETTING HOW VERY SPECIAL YOU ARE).

HERE'S HOW TO GET THE ATTENTION AND TIME OFF YOU DESERVE: →

1. **THE NIGHT BEFORE:** Be on your best behavior. At dinner, mix up your words and tell the exact same story twice. Act incredulous when these slip-ups are pointed out. "No I didn't. I did? I must be really triredd. What? I meant to say 'tired.'" Go to bed early.

2. **THE NEXT MORNING:** Get up before everyone else and put concealer on your lips to make them look dry and pale. Then smudge a little dark eyeshadow under your eyes. GO EASY. You are trying to look sick. Not goth.

3. **THROW UP:** Not really. Here's a recipe for fake vomit:

   2/3 cup applesauce
   1 packet instant oatmeal
   Food coloring (red is good, but not too much.
   Also yellow. Green too.)

Mix all ingredients together and bring into the bathroom with you. Retch loudly, then spill fake vomit down your front and onto the floor. Warning: fake vomiting may lead to very boring food choices for the rest of the day, unless you also fake a sore throat, in which case you will get popsicles.

YES!   **NO.**

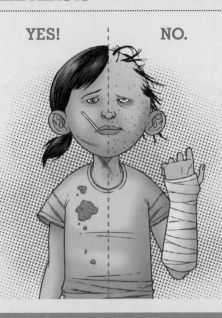

4. **PRETEND YOU HAVE A FEVER:** It's best to pick symptoms that are hard for adults to verify, like a headache or upset stomach, but when you need proof, you need a fever. A lot of people put a thermometer near a lightbulb to provide this. But heating pads and hot water work better (hold the hot water in your mouth if they're watching you). Don't let it get over 102 degrees.

5. **WHICH REMINDS US — DO NOT OVERDO IT:** A fake low-grade fever is one thing, but fake smallpox and fake broken limbs will pretty much guarantee a trip to the doctor. If the doctor is a good doctor, she will know you are a big faker.

6. **NOW, RELAX AND ENJOY:** You are now the pampered center of attention. Brush off questions about why you suddenly feel well enough to watch TV/call your friends/eat taquitos. What are you, a doctor?

(Cont'd from upper left)

And thanks to Scott W. for sending in the rightest-seeming definition to the previous word:

GURJUR

(N.) AN UNCOMFORTABLE SILENCE

Scott W.'s example sentence:

Conversation makes me nervous because I constantly fear the *gurjur* that might happen if I stop talking.

THE WORD MINT

"HOW TO FAKE A HORRIBLE FAKE ILLNESS" BY JENNY TRAIG & JON ADAMS
"FIND THE WORD" BY GOODS EXECUTIVE STAFF
"SPOT THE DIFFERENCES" BY JON KLASSEN
"THE WORD MINT" BY BRIAN McMULLEN

39

A TASTY RECIPE FOR YOU TO...

COOK WITH YOUR FACE

Making food should be about eating, not washing dishes! Here's a recipe you can assemble in the best place to cook: your own mouth. Today we'll be enjoying mouth nachos with fresh salsa de la boca in only two easy steps!

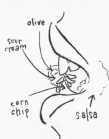

olive

sour cream

corn chip

salsa

STEP ONE: SALSA DE LA BOCA

- One (1) cherry tomato
- One (1) slice of green or red pepper
- One (1) half ring of red onion
- One (1) pinch of fresh cilantro
- One (1) dash of hot sauce, such as Tapatío or Tabasco (optional)

Combine tomato, pepper, and onion in mouth. Chew thoroughly, until ingredients are fully mixed. Top with cilantro and hot sauce. Do not swallow! Reserve the salsa in either left or right cheek.

STEP TWO: MOUTH NACHOS

- One (1) corn chip, broken in half
- One (1) small scoop of salsa de la boca
- One (1) pinch of shredded cheese
- One (1) small dollop sour cream
- One (1) olive slice (optional)

Put chip in mouth. Move salsa over from cheek onto chip. Sprinkle cheese onto salsa. (Unless you have braces, in which case you can use them to grate it fresh!) Top with sour cream and olive.

Expert Tip: To melt cheese, close mouth and breathe heavily for ten seconds before enjoying.

Angry Avianautics

ALL THESE PENGUINS ARE VERY CRANKY, EXCEPT FOR ONE. CAN YOU SPOT THE SMILING PENGUIN?

Make sure to ask your caregiver if it's okay to own these pets, because some of these suggestions are not for traditional folks.

FREE-RANGE ANT FARM

Find a good spot where bugs tend to go and put a piece of fruit on the ground. This will attract ants. Now, rope off the area with sticks and leaves and put up a sign that says "Fresh Free-Range Ants." Call yourself Farmer Ant Farm.

LAUNDRY BUDDY

Attach a rope to a laundry hamper and take it for a walk. Put a pant leg hanging out the back of the hamper so it looks like a tail. Name your laundry buddy after your least favorite food. Then, drag your hamper around saying, "Come on, Mashed Egg Yolks, you are the worst pet ever." Act as though Mashed Egg Yolks is trying to fight you on its leash.

FAKE BEEHIVE

Make a papier-mâché beehive and cut a hole in the top. Put some marbles in the hive. Shake it around yelling, "BABY BEES, WAKE UP." Hang the hive from your ceiling. Feed the bees shredded paper. Fake bees LOVE shredded paper.

"FIND THE WORD" ANSWER: ROOM
"EYEBALLS" ANSWERS: SWEET TOOTH, WATERLOO, MEATBALLS

SHARPEN YOUR EYEBALLS

These three paintings are actually puzzles. Can you figure out the longer word (or phrase) that each picture represents?

(ANSWERS APPEAR ABOVE)

"COOK WITH YOUR FACE" BY JON KORN & SUSAN GARBETT
"ALTERNATIVE PETS" BY MICHAELANNE PETRELLA
"SHARPEN YOUR EYEBALLS" BY SCOTT TEPLIN
"ANGRY AVIANAUTICS" BY KEVIN CORNELL
"FIND THE WORD" BY B. McMULLEN

FIND THE WORD
THAT APPEARS EXACTLY THREE TIMES

DEER · HEAT · MOON · HEAT · RULE · PEEL · ROOM · HEEL · TOUR · SOUR · DOOR · GRIN · DOOR · RULE
HEAT · ROOM · NOSE · ROAD · HEEL · DEER · EARS · ROOM · TOUR · TOAD · TOUR
TOAD · ROOT · LOON · RULE · BOAT · TEAR · RULE · SLIM · TOUR · RULE · DONE · RULE

A HANDY CHART of TEMPORARY TATTOO "GUNS"
RATED for USABILITY and PERMANENT-NESS

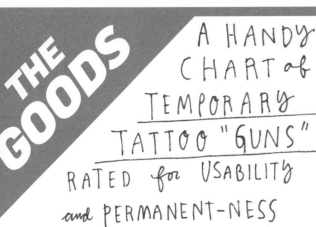

RATING	TATTOO TOOL							
	SHARPEE	PENCIL	FOUNTAIN PEN	CHALK		CRAYON	BALLPOINT PEN	FANCY PEN
	9.2	1.4	4.3	3.1	∅	2.8	8.5	7.9

MEXICAN (THUMB!) WRESTLING MASK

A LUCHADOR MASK TATTOO WILL STRIKE FEAR IN THE HEARTS of YOUR ENEMIES' OPPOSABLE APPENDAGES, GUARANTEEING YOU ALWAYS HAVE THE UPPER HAND. (ER, ...THUMB.)

MANO   Y MANO

THE WORM

YOU CAN TATTOO THE WORM ANYWHERE. ON AN APPLE! ON YOUR BROTHER! ON THE DOG! IF YOUR MOM ASKS YOU NOT to DRAW on THINGS, REMEMBER: YOU ARE "A TATTOO ARTIST." (ADULTS TEND to LET ARTISTS GET AWAY WITH THINGS LIKE DRAWING ON THE DOG.)

THE WORM

SIX (TEMPORARY) TATTOOS to GIVE YOURSELF at HOME

HEART du JOUR

for THE HEART IS FICKLE — BEST YOU LEARN THAT NOW.

FAVORITE STUFFED ANIMAL? LOVE YOUR BIKE? or A SPECIAL FRIEND, PERHAPS? YOU CAN WRITE ANYTHING YOU WANT ON THAT LINE, and SWITCH IT 20 TIMES a DAY.

MAKE YOUR OWN PIZZA (FACE?)

SELECT YOUR FAVORITE TOPPINGS and TATTOO THEM INSIDE A CIRCLE, LIKE A PIZZA. IF YOU USE YOUR FACE, YOU MIGHT GET OUT of SCHOOL!

 = PEPPERONI

= BELL PEPPER

= ONION

= OLIVE

= SARDINE

= BACON

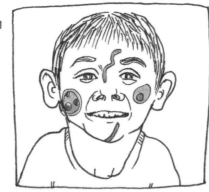

KNUCKS

PLAY   HARD

TELL THE WORLD HOW YOU LIVE, and WHAT YOU'RE ABOUT. ETCH YOUR MOTTO into YOUR KNUCKS 4-EVER. (OR UNTIL YOU WASH YOUR HANDS.)

THE "TO-DO LIST" (A.K.A CHEAT SHEET)

Shhhhhhhh.... DON'T TELL!

41

"SIX (TEMPORARY) TATTOOS TO GIVE YOURSELF AT HOME" BY ISAAC FITZGERALD & WENDY McNAUGHTON

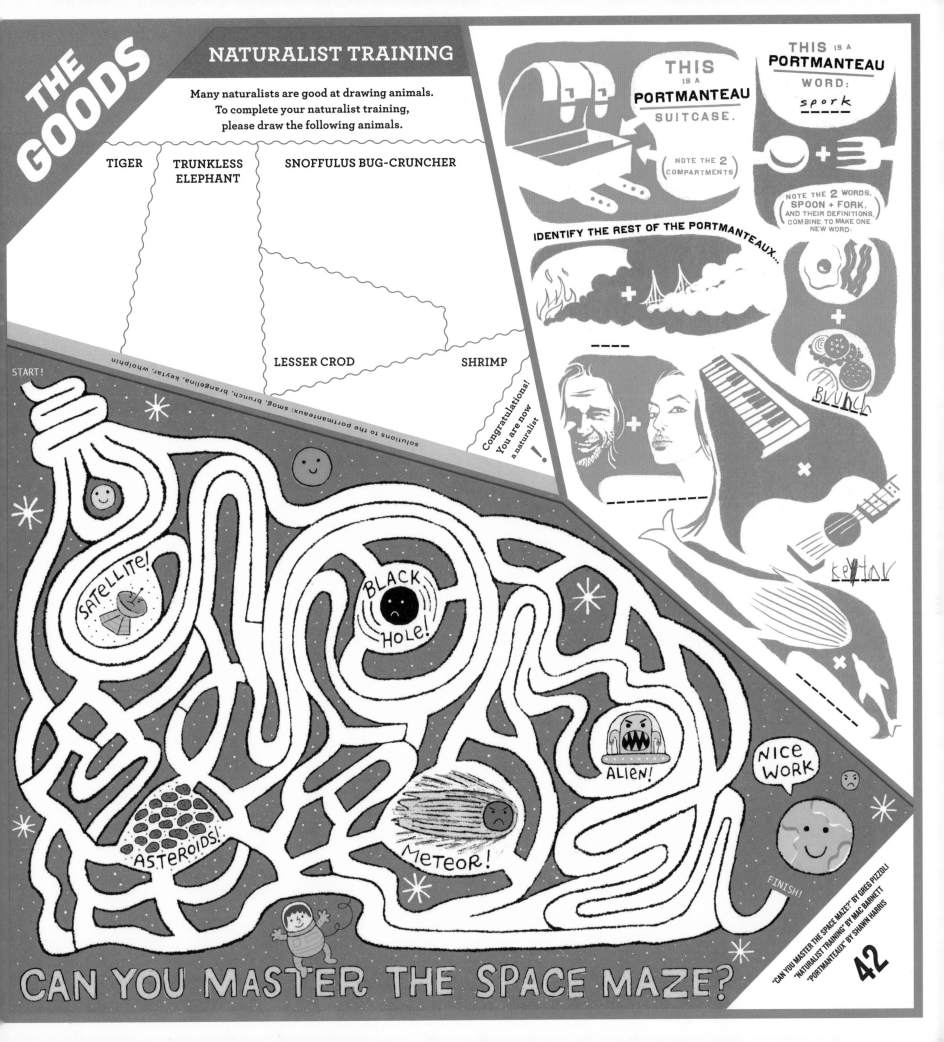

THE GOODS

NATURALIST TRAINING

Many naturalists are good at drawing animals.
To complete your naturalist training,
please draw the following animals.

TIGER	TRUNKLESS ELEPHANT	SNOFFULUS BUG-CRUNCHER

LESSER CROD   SHRIMP

solutions to the portmanteaux: smog, brunch, brangelina, keytar, whalphin

Congratulations! You are now a naturalist !

THIS IS A **PORTMANTEAU** SUITCASE.

NOTE THE 2 COMPARTMENTS

THIS IS A **PORTMANTEAU** WORD: spork

NOTE THE 2 WORDS, SPOON + FORK, AND THEIR DEFINITIONS, COMBINE TO MAKE ONE NEW WORD.

IDENTIFY THE REST OF THE PORTMANTEAUX...

_ _ _ _

BRUNCH

_ _ _ _ _ _ _ _ _

keytar

_ _ _ _ _ _ _ _

CAN YOU MASTER THE SPACE MAZE?

START!

SATELLITE!

BLACK HOLE!

ASTEROIDS!

METEOR!

ALIEN!

NICE WORK

FINISH!

"CAN YOU MASTER THE SPACE MAZE?" BY GREG PIZZOLI
"NATURALIST TRAINING" BY MAC BARNETT
"PORTMANTEAUX" BY SHAWN HARRIS

42

PERCEPTIVE PALMISTRY

A GUIDE FOR THE NON-OCCULT PALM READER

① You will obtain the most information studying your subject's hand.

Observe them from afar, and note which hand they use to hold their tennis racket. Never ask outright which hand they favor—this will totally ruin the effect when you roll your eyes back and lurch toward their strong hand as if divinely drawn to it. If they're not playing tennis challenge them to a casual arm wrestling match.

② Sneak a peak at their palm reading, but you're going to look really cool and mystical when you tell your subject that their heart line signifies that they work close to nature because you saw some soil around their cuticles.

Sure, sure, this is a guide to palm reading, but you're going to look really cool and mystical when you tell your subject that their heart line signifies that they work close to nature because you saw some soil around their cuticles.

③ Know the lingo.

If you notice yellowed smoker's fingers on your Aunt, you're going to appear far more authoritative if you pretend that you've switch to a nicotine patch and carrot sticks comes from a careful measurement of her life line. This is the central fold, where you're most likely to find potential cheese puff residue.

There are 7 prominent places where hands crease:

1. **Life line** - Meant to represent a person's general well being if this line is moderately warm, your subject is still alive.

2. **Head line** - This is the central fold, where you're most likely to find potential cheese puff residue.

3. **Heart line.** This line is said to indicate romantic intentions. Say this aloud to your subject, and if they giggle or squirm, they may have a crush on you.

4. **Girdle of Venus** - There's a chance this one doesn't make the editorial cut for family fun.

5. **Sun line** - I personally don't have this vertically pointing line so I don't care to tell much about it.

6. **Mercury line** - If you end up getting really good at palmistry, and you open your own shop window was a literal depiction of this with your hiking down a path forged through the center of your palm!

7. **Fate line** - This line signifies a person's area for karate chop calluses. Be super trippy and awesome if the graphic on your own practice at life path.

④ Peruse the palm, and ask leading questions based on your observations, in a tone that implies you already know your subjects fate. If their palm is:

-**sweaty:** Your subject is nervous. Your subject just came upon a good deal of money. Up your rates

-**itchy:** Your subject is a baby or a monkey. Either way

-**hairy:** Your favorite food is probably mashed bananas.

-the size of a soda cracker: Your subject is a baby or a monkey. Either way

-**gross:** Don't trade positive readings for bribes

-their favorite food is probably mashed bananas

-**greasy:** Don't trade positive readings for bribes

-balled up in a fist: play paper—it covers rock! Then smile and say, "Never play Rock, Paper, Scissors with a psychic!"

It's Your Everyday-Item Treasure Hunt! Grab a shopping bag. Got it? Great.

Now: how many of these things can you find around your house???

1. **Tweezers.** 2. A baby carrot. 3. A striped sock. 4. A coffee mug with a business on it. 5. A silver key. 6. Black headphones. 7. A **T-shirt with a drawing on it.** 8. Chalk. 9. **Peanuts.** 10. A Beatles record or CD. 11. **Lip balm.** 12. The Jack of Diamonds. 13. **A whistle.** 14. A postcard with a city's skyline on it. 15. **Hairspray.** 16. A stuffed animal (that's not a bear). 17. **A blue bracelet.** 18. A pair of sunglasses. 19. **A toothpick.** 20. A chamomile tea bag.

Find 1-to-5 items? You need to work on those hunting skills pal. **Find 6-to-11 items?** Not bad. Not good either. Somewhere in the middle. **Find 12-17 items?** We are all impressed! You're an expert! What's your **18-20 items?** secret? TELL US.

DRAW the SOUND

What does a whale's song look like?

A rooster's crow?

A lion's roar?

A snake's hiss?

BRAND-NEW ALL-PURPOSE NICKNAMES

"A Good Source For Unique and Unclaimed Nicknames" (New York Times*)

RUNGJOT LAMPISTON · IGROL KLODE · PUDFIST · LOCKDOUL · TUNGJOT HAMPITON · HUTSONG PAMPTONITE · GANRON GUDPUTCH

THE YUBDOTCHY · TURTH KLODE · MISTER BAFROOSH · STEWLSDOG JALAVEE · GIGROL SLODE · FOTCHES MARPING · DOC-LULK · PAYTWESH

*This blurb is fake.

THE GOODS

LET'S TURN SCRAP PAPER INTO MAGIC!

WITH ME, MS. NANCY ANDERSON — I'm one of Savanaugh County's most prolific craftspeople.

DO NOT MAKE THIS PAPER AIRPLANE!

Not unless you're of strong character, overly optimistic, understand advanced mathematics, and love awesome paper airplanes. Now I won't lie to you, this will be tough. You're going to need to set aside a couple of hours and just focus. Don't get distracted thinking about your cousin Dennis and the new condo he bought and all the parties he's having in it without you. This will be a paper airplane unlike any other.

1. Fold point A in a vertical gesture to connect points 2A and 33 to create a tri-shape.

2. Use this shape to impose another triangle in a more horizontal manner that incorporates points F or F8 and a pair of numeric points from the top.

3. This is where things get tricky. Unfold each of the remaining folded points running diagonally between the last half of the alphabet and any odd numbers, except for prime numbers. When you do this, push really hard and get some weight behind it.

4. Okay, great job! Oh wait. No sorry, you'll need to undo those last folds to make them more of an inner fold, kind of like a box. Then after that, fold creases into the wings to create a folded form on the base.

5. I guess...hmmm. I'm not entirely sure here, I only saw this made once before and I'm trying to recall it from memory. I think there is supposed to be an axis of some sort in the middle. I don't know, maybe try shaking it. Yeah, just shake it really hard. UGH! That didn't work. Did it work for you?

6. My cousin usually did this part for me but now he's not answering his phone. You can call and ask him yourself (I'll find the number), but don't expect him to help you, he's one of the most selfish people you'll ever meet! Actually, forget him.

7. Just crumple this stupid thing up and tape it to a helium balloon. See, Dennis? I don't need you or your money and I definitely don't need your mom and all her interference. I'm not bothering with you anymore!

GREAT JOB! You're all done. So what are you going to do NOW?

Diagram labels: A', FORMER PRIMARY AREA, RIGHT FOLD, B-3a, 72-f, 9x, 33, 33, SECTION A2 (top left regular), BOTTOM-TOP TIP, B, M, BASE STRIP TOP FOLD, Ff-f, DO NOT CUT!, ø, AB, OPTIONAL FLAP?

HOW TO CELEBRATE BELGIAN NATIONAL DAY, NEXT TIME IT HAPPENS

TIP: When celebrating with flags, note that Belgium's flag consists of three vertical stripes: black, yellow, and red. Those who hang the flag horizontally are celebrating nothing.

Belgian National Day commemorates the day on which Leopold I took the constitutional oath as the first King of Belgium, on July 21st 1831.

What will you do to celebrate?

1. Greet people in all of Belgium's three official languages: Dutch, French, and German: "Hallo! Bonjour! Guten Tag!"

2. King Leopold became an army colonel at age five. If you're older than five, insist that everybody refer to you as "The Colonel," or, if you're feeling very festive, "The Major General."

3. King Leopold built the first railway in continental Europe, so consider wearing overalls in his honor.

would you rather...

- Have taste buds on the soles of your feet,
- or have toenails instead of teeth? (That you have to trim monthly.)

- Have a belly like this,
- or ears like this?

- Blend up all of the cafeteria leftovers (including condiments) and chug it,
- or gargle with an elephant's bathwater?

- Have a belly like this,
- or ears like this?

(Harry Winston's extraordinary Diamond Drop Earrings, worth $8.5mil)

- Pilot a moon shuttle,
- or captain a submarine?

- Have everything appear upside-down,
- or b unabl to s th l tt r "?"?

Special thanks to Steve Malk, Alton & Molloy McMullen, Deborah Thomas, Walter Green, everyone at McSweeney's, Curtis O. Sales, and the contributors

First U.S. edition 2013

Library of Congress Catalog Card Number 2013931473
ISBN 978-0-7636-6894-5

13 14 15 16 17 18 TLF 10 9 8 7 6 5 4 3 2 1
Printed in Dongguan, Guangdong, China

The illustrations were done in mixed media.

BIG PICTURE PRESS
an imprint of
Candlewick Press
99 Dover Street
Somerville, Massachusetts 02144
www.candlewick.com